THE GRACE OF SAVING

The Inspiring Story of America's Smartest Shopper

By Teri Gault and Paul Joseph Gulino

I dedicate this book to my Dad who now sings in the choir of angels, and my mom, who's sitting on the front porch of her gorgeous southern mansion, with a mint julep, and will have one for me when I get there. – Teri Gault

Table of Contents

Acknowledgements

I would like to thank God for giving me His best, starting with my grandparents, my mom, and my dad who modeled the grace of saving, and encouraged, prayed, and believed in me. And my sister, Karen, who slaves daily with her hand to the plow, and always avails her sister's heart to me, my best friend for all eternity. And Greg for not only believing in me, but lifting me up when I was down, and always telling me that what I was building would snowball and be a blessing to millions, and I'm so thankful he was right. And my sons, Joe and Christian, even while young and growing up, understood, supported, encouraged, appreciated and respected the business I was building, and despite the fact that it took me away from them, they contributed to the journey that we were on together. And Heather, my daughter in law, amazing, brilliant and wiser than her years, for giving up four years to work her tail off on the road with and for her mother in law! And my right hand man, corporate attorney, Richie, who is like a brother to me, caught the vision, carries the torch, never fails me, and never will. And the amazingly gifted Paul, for sitting for hours and hours with me, and weaving my story so beautifully. And last but not least, my wonderful, dedicated, cream of the crop staff who've given their best day in and day out. I pray that all of these dear ones are blessed infinitely beyond their highest prayers, desires, thoughts or hopes.

1. The Peach Seed Monkey

Our family never had a tradition of the passing on of wealth from one generation to the next. We had traditions, but not the wealth. We were Oklahomans of many generations, and worked with our hands, on farms and in simple labor, and wealth was not easy to come by. We can trace our roots from before the time when the Boomers and the Sooners violated Indian land in 1889, for my great grandmother was herself a Choctaw Indian, one of those so violated. Our family survived by thrift, through some very lean times. Choctaw Indians certainly knew thrift—they were a nomadic people, who carried all earthly possessions with them as they went.

Appropriate to this humble background was our family's most central tradition, that of the "Peach Seed Monkey." It began during the Great Depression of the 1930s, which coincided with severe drought in Oklahoma, kicking up a storm of hunger, deprivation and desperation known as the *Dust Bowl*. In those days, the central obsessions of my Grand-Mommy and Grand-Daddy were food and shelter for themselves and their only child—my father. All other concerns were afterthoughts. It was a particularly cold and bleak December, and my family's economic privation even threatened the arrival of Santa Claus. My Grand-Daddy averted this looming disaster through his ingenuity, fashioning delightful toys for my father in his workshop, from

1

materials gathered from the discards and scrap metal in the nearby lumber yard, finished off with a coat of brightly colored paint.

When Christmas day dawned that year, my father was thrilled, but my Grand-Daddy belatedly realized Santa had neglected my Grand-Mommy. He quietly slipped away in mid-afternoon back to his workshop, where he remained for several hours. As dinner time approached, my Grand-Mommy went out back to find out what he was up to, and discovered him at his workbench, bending over a small object with his carving knife.

"What are you doing?" she said, startling him.

My Grand-Daddy, caught in the act, had little choice but to come clean.

"Carving a monkey."

"A what?" my Grand-Mommy asked, looking over his shoulder. There it was—no more than an inch high—a small brown monkey. "Where did you get that?"

"From a tree, where else?" my Grand-Daddy said.

"Lyndon," said my Grand-Mommy, frowning.

"From a tree, I tell you. A peach tree. I carved it from a peach seed."

My Grand-Mommy looked at it again, and could now see, with astonishment, how skillfully he had rendered the form of a monkey out of a craggy pit.

"Seems Santa was a bit forgetful this year, and so I thought I'd help him out. It was supposed to be a surprise, but as long as you know, you may as well help. Hold it while I glue the eyes on."

He handed the monkey to Grand-Mommy, then took hold of one of two small glittery stones on the workbench.

"Where did you get the diamonds?" my Grand-Mommy asked, pretty sure they were fake but afraid he might've done something foolish.

My Grand-Daddy growled. "I chipped them off a piece of glass. Now hold still!"

With this, he carefully glued the two eyes on, and the peach seed monkey had the gift of sight. My Grand-Daddy smiled and presented it to my Grand-Mommy with a kiss.

I don't know how long my Grand-Daddy had contemplated making a monkey from a peach seed, whether he'd read about it or seen it done somewhere, or if it had occurred to him on a whim in his workshop that morning. Likewise, I don't know if he'd imagined it would last more than a day or so, delicate as it was, with my father and his rambunctious friends in the house and a wife who had much on her mind besides caring for a small and inconsequential gift.

But for some reason, that monkey lived on with us. It found its way into a small cardboard box, insulated with cotton, and my Grand-Mommy kept it with her most cherished possessions. Even as the years grew less lean, she treasured it, perhaps as a reminder of what love could accomplish when material things were scarce.

Each Christmas eve when I was young, my Grand-Mommy would gather us around her knee and retell us the story of that bleak Christmas day long ago, when the warmth and love of a man made something of nothing. At the end of the telling, she would open the small box for the "showing" of the peach seed monkey, and we'd take turns holding it, our little hands cradling it carefully while our faces lit up with joy and wonder.

Grand-Mommy would quietly observe us admiring the family treasure, and after a few moments, she would inevitably exclaim, "Just imagine! He carved that out of a peach seed!"

We children got to know the story by heart, but each time we heard it retold, we felt it was as alive and vivid as the first time. In later years, my Grand-Mommy passed the peach seed monkey on to me, and I would retell the story for my children, and just two years ago I passed it along to my eldest son Joe.

Many things have changed since I first set eyes on the Peach Seed Monkey, surrounded by family in the warmth of a Christmas holiday. Things have grown more complex. I have cycled through periods of richness and poverty, and now, as I have come into the possession of valuable earthly things, I still see the value in that simplest of gifts, and I see it has lost none of its worth.

During the Great Depression my Grand-Daddy took that which was discarded—the seed of a fruit whose meat had been eaten, and two bits of glass that would provide no window nor protect anyone from the cold—and used them to create a lasting wealth he could hardly have foreseen. During the time of my own family's trials, I likewise took what many might thoughtlessly discard—the supermarket flyers from newspapers, and a few hours on Sunday mornings—and used them to create and share with others a different kind of wealth, a wealth that comes through the simple act of saving.

I think there is beauty in taking something right in front of us— something we see every day, yet hardly notice—and using it in a new and innovative way to help families.

This is the story of the fat times and lean, of humble beginnings, soaring prosperity, and bumpy landings which forced me to see, in the tradition of the peach seed monkey, how to live.

2. Altus

  I can remember a bus, traveling across great expanses of desert. Not Oklahoma; no, further west. Oklahoma is a fertile place, not a desert place.

  I can remember music, too. Both traveling and music are in my earliest memories.

  I was born in Enid, Oklahoma, and grew up in Altus, almost exactly one thousand miles from each coast, where U.S. Route 283 comes down from the forbidding rangeland of west Oklahoma and meets Route 62 heading in from Lawton, a small town whose chief characteristic for us was that it was bigger than our small town.

  We came to settle in that uncertain perch in the midst of vastness because my father, a minister just a few years out of Southwestern Theological Seminary in Fort Worth, Texas, was looking for a flock, and Altus needed a shepherd. And more than that—it needed a shepherd who knew music, and my father had a lifelong love of music, holding a Master of Church Music degree. He was in fact the greatest baritone God ever made. That may sound biased, but it's true, I swear it.

  So my father jumped at the chance of taking the open position of youth minister/music director, and we jumped with him, and made our life there, in a sea of undulating rangeland, with an occasional hillock, pond or stand of trees to break up the horizon.

When my father took his position, he had two items on his agenda—securing the souls of those he served, and securing the voices of as many of them as possible. During his studies at the university, he and his classmates shared a common goal: to lead the largest music program in whatever state they wound up in. My father, in taking the position in the small town of Altus, had his work cut out for him.

"How can you do it here?" I remember my mother asking him, in her distinctive South Carolina twang. We had just taken our first tour of the town, after my father had accepted the post, a tour that had lasted all of ten minutes, encompassing the length of Broadway and Main. "We've been banished to this outpost."

"We'll manage. It will be a challenge, but—"

"You can't make a choir out of the blades of grass, and I don't see much of anything else here."

"The last chapter hasn't been written yet," said my father, trying hard to convey wisdom way beyond his years.

"The *last* chapter?" my mother asked. "I'm worried about *this* one!"

I quickly volunteered my younger sister Karen and I. We were age three and five, respectively.

"There," my father smiled. "I haven't even started yet and I've already doubled the size of the choir."

Actually, things were not as dire as my mother imagined. Altus had a small population but a big church; it only needed someone who was both passionate about music and full of energy, and my father was both.

When I was five his choir program numbered a hundred; by my eighth birthday there were over six hundred members in twelve choirs, from pre-school to seniors, eight to twelve ensemble groups, various youth and adult choirs, and even a rock band. My father had the satisfaction of besting his peers, because his music program had indeed become the largest of any church in the state of Oklahoma.

Which is where my memory of music comes from.

It was in the air; it permeated all we did, seven days a week. I sang in the youth choir, helped my father when he penned musicals, and appeared in some of those. By the spring of my sixth year, the little town of Altus couldn't hold all the music my father had to give, and it spilled forth across the southwest.

Which is where my memory of the bus comes in.

When I was six, my father received a letter from the minister of a church in Glorieta, New Mexico, inviting him to bring his youth choir for a guest performance during the summer. This was quickly followed by similar invitations from churches in Albuquerque. My father's fame was spreading, and spreading westward.

From the moment I learned that our choir was leaving on a summer tour out west, and that I'd be going, I could hardly sleep. My role was to be a modest one—turning the pages of the sheet music for the pianist—but I rehearsed it carefully with him in the weeks leading up to our departure. I wanted everything to be perfect!

Those weeks were also filled with a frenzy of fundraising activity on the part of all the youth music members. Fortunately the fundraising was fun, because my father had a way of making everything fun.

My favorite fundraising method was a game called *Bigger and Better*. For this, we'd break up into teams of about four, and each team started out with a paper clip, and went door to door and. "We're on a bigger and better hunt," we'd say. "Do you have anything you will give us for this paper clip that is bigger and better?" At each house, people would donate something more valuable; each time, we'd tell the donor that we'd started out with a mere paper clip to inspire them, and urge them to help us: the team that wound up with the most valuable donation would be declared the winner and get free tickets to an amusement park.

As the trips became a yearly experience, so too did the fundraising. That first year, our team ended up with a working record player, and we thought we'd won, until we returned to the church, and discovered that one team had an antique claw-footed bathtub in pretty good shape.

That team was pretty happy until one more late-arriving group showed up—in a car! It was a beat up jalopy that barely ran, but it ran well enough for the team to get to the church and claim the prize. Turned out, they had traded up to a power tool the last donor really wanted, and the donor happened to be keen on getting rid of his jalopy, so the deal was done.

It was pure small town Americana, and that is, of course, exactly where it took place.

When the big day arrived, my mother awoke to find me already dressed and sleeping by the door, where I'd spent the night, making sure I was ready when it was time to leave.

I'm sure I slept some on the bus as we vaulted across the plains westward, but I'm equally sure that I fought sleep with every ounce of strength a six year old could muster. I was with a busload of teenagers, infected by their manic energy and intrigued by their mysterious, grown-up ways. I was excited too by what was going on outside the bus—the topography changing from what I knew so well to what I'd never seen—canyons, mountains, scrub, desert sands. I was thrilled by the changes in the human topography as well—discovering with our house visits how others lived in their enclaves, the endless variations of family and relationships, of the different churches, and singing styles, the various audiences.

Always, it seemed, the unexpected experiences were the best. One of these occurred during an unscheduled stop in Peach Springs, Arizona on old Route 66 when we were en route to points west. We had engine trouble, so my Dad pulled the bus into that little town, where we had to wait for parts. As evening came on, people began to gather around to find out who we were.

My father saw an opportunity in the growing crowd. We had stopped in front of the post office, which had an electric outlet just inside the main door.

"Let's give them a show!" he shouted.

We quickly unloaded all the equipment and instruments, and plugged in the amplifiers, and proceeded to set the crowd on fire. We played into the night, slept in the post office, and were on our way they next morning. What began as a frustrating mechanical failure left me with long lasting memories of the appreciative townspeople, their smiling faces lit up in the wash of headlights and a bright desert moon, and the joy we had on our impromptu stage, sharing the gifts of song and music in a place that had expected neither.

I did a lot of singing in those days, but acting was in my blood, too. My debut occurred at age five, when I re-enacted the Christmas story for my parents, playing the role of Joseph to three-year-old Karen's Mary, with the cat standing in as the Christ child (aside from some inopportune purring on the part of the baby Jesus, we pulled it off with a good deal of enthusiasm if not scriptural authenticity).

My tendency toward theatricality actually predates this debut, though; in fact, I trace it to the birth of Karen, when I was two. Karen was so beautiful: big blue eyes and a precious little face—quiet, sweet, and adorable—that she didn't have to do anything to get attention, even from strangers. I felt myself pushed into the periphery of my parents' attention, and did whatever I could to fight back.

When my father aimed our home movie camera on Karen, I would barge in and strike a ridiculous pose, like a movie star or glamour girl. I was a tall, gangly, skinny little girl, with an obnoxious habit of pestering anyone in Karen's presence for attention. Somewhat remarkably, I don't have any memories of anyone ever telling me that I was obnoxious or undesirable. I always felt that my antics were effective and acceptable, which suggests I was loved—and forgiven— to a greater extent than I'd imagined.

During the spring of my seventh year, my father received invitations from various churches in the west, and the year after that, one arrived from a church in Anaheim, California.

California.

It was the first time the word had entered my life. I knew nothing of the place, but the excitement my mother had at the mention of its name in turn filled me with excitement. As news spread among the youth choir that we'd be going to California, this excitement was amplified by the energies of a hundreds of teenagers, and their thrill became my own. I didn't know where or what it was, but I could only imagine that California was a good place.

Before we left early one Monday morning in early summer 1968, my father had to overcome one major difficulty: luggage overload. The teenage girls felt it necessary to bring enough outfits and shoes to fill two buses, and we had only one, and that one had to carry people as well as luggage.

I remember vividly the means he used to dispose of the problem: he had all the girls line up in the parking lot at the front end of the bus and, using a stopwatch, made them rush to the rear of the bus with as much luggage as they could carry, within one minute. Whatever they couldn't get across the finish line in time would remain in Altus. In one stroke, my father had accomplished three things: cutting down the luggage to a manageable amount, giving the girls plenty of exercise, and making it all fun—at least for those of us watching. In later tours, the event became more elaborate. My father would bring a loudspeaker and announce it like a sportscaster, identifying the girls he knew so well by their nicknames and particular characteristics. It had become a joyful ritual, heralding the arrival of another adventure out west.

As I think back on that first journey to California from Altus, I can't help but think that God had drama in mind when he laid out the landscape, at least to a person heading from east to west. You begin where all is flat and predictable, then the scenery becomes gradually more extreme—by turns hotter and colder, higher and lower, more jagged, more exotic. Finally at the climax of the journey you arrive in California, emerging triumphant through the San Gabriel Mountains, skirting what to the north are both the lowest point (Death Valley) and highest point (Mount Whitney) in the Continental United States, and hurtle southwestward as the Southern California cities of San Bernardino and Los Angeles opened up before you. At last you come to rest by the cooling breeze of some of the most beautiful beaches on earth, populated by palm trees and friendly smiles: a happy ending.

The first thing I noticed about California was the palm trees. Exotic.

The second thing was the beach. A blast.

The palm trees were everywhere to behold. The beach was not *quite* everywhere, but the day after our first concert we were all invited to a beautiful beachfront home for a swim party. It was the coolest thing ever. When we concluded our stay in Anaheim, the young people at the church were so enthusiastic they followed us in their cars, honking and waving, as far as San Bernardino—fifty miles—before they finally turned around to go back home.

Thus, my first impressions of California were of beauty in its land and its people, the joy with which they received us and the appreciative hosts and audiences they made. I remember the pristine parks and playgrounds, tearing around the jungle gyms, dipping my feet in the cooling waves of the Pacific.

That was in Anaheim.

My second impression involved leather jackets, tattoos, drugs, and alcohol.

That was on the Sunset Strip.

One of the invitations my father had received the spring before our first California trip was from a man named Arthur Blessitt, who ran a soup kitchen that ministered primarily to Hell's Angels and other bikers in what was, curiously, one of the glamorous areas of Los Angeles. The Sunset Strip bisects the Hollywood Hills to the north and West Hollywood to the south, and touches Beverly Hills at its western most point. The pressure of all this material wealth comes to bear harshly on this one section, with its glitz and bright lights, and human beings, for all their appearances, are soft and frail, and no match for the grinding stress such a culture can put on them. Amidst the movie stars and tourists there was prostitution, drugs, thievery and despair.

So it was with the populace of bikers Blessitt ministered to, many of whom found their brawny physical demeanors inadequate, and bolstered themselves with drugs and alcohol, and ran through their money, and came to us as beggars.

One in particular I befriended.

It was one of those early July afternoons in California, with a pale sun that looked colder than it really was shining down and

12

obliterating the nuances of color on the Strip, bathing everything in milky hues. I was in the prep room, a big rustic space with long counters and an industrial-strength stove, helping my sister and mother set out bread and cheese on trays. My mother asked me to go out to the storage room to get some bottles of juice, and when I got there, I was confronted by numerous flavor choices, and decided to take as many as I could carry. I stuffed them into a big canvas sack and attempted, in vain, to lift it. I opted to drag it across the floor.

As I labored with my burden through the main serving room, where the bikers were arriving, a deep voice posed a simple question to me:

"Need a hand there?"

The hand being offered to me was probably the biggest I'd ever seen; it belonged to a man they called Lerch, whose arms were about as thick as I was, heavily populated with tattoos, and whose body was big enough to block the sunshine coming in through the plate glass window.

"I could truly use one, sir," I replied. What else could I say? It was the truth.

He grinned, and lifted the sack easily with one hand, then lifted me with the other, and carried us both to the prep room, where my mother and sister greeted me with an alarmed look in their eyes.

Lerch surely was an alarming figure, between his stature, shaved head, chains and leather, but for some reason he never frightened me. He became a regular at the soup kitchen, and I never hesitated to ask him for help with any burden I had, whether it was hauling food stocks or cutting up meat or bread. Maybe my simple trust and faith in him disarmed him; I don't know. But we'd not only work on food together in the kitchen, but we'd also play games, and talk, and he'd share stories about life on the road, and I'd share my more humble stories of play in Altus.

He remained a fixture in my mind even after we left, and I thought about him and hoped that he would overcome whatever difficulties he had. When we returned in subsequent years, he was always there, and always remembered me.

Intruding into these experiences, and providing a backdrop that perhaps—by its sinister contrast—intensified my moments of joy—was a trauma my mother suffered. When I was five, she became suddenly ill and we took her to a hospital in neighboring Lawton. The diagnosis was *pancreatitis*, a disorder that is usually treated easily with medication, but in rare cases can be chronic, life-threatening, and require extended hospital stays.

Unfortunately, my mother suffered from the chronic variety.

The attacks would come suddenly, and would result in long hospital stays—frequently months at a time. Often the condition is associated with alcohol use, but in my mother's case it was not—she rarely drank. During these intervals of illness, my father often had to travel to other churches for long stretches, and my sister and I would be left in the care of various friends and parishioners, compounding our anxiety. The families with whom we were sheltered did their best, but they had lives of their own, and we often felt lost, like unnoticed shadows in forgotten corners and hallways.

And sometimes the families could be downright insensitive. On one occasion, when my sister and I were placed in different homes—a rare but not unknown situation—the family with whom I was placed set the dinner table with nothing but bread and water, and the father made a remark about how it was prison food. It was some sort of ill-advised joke meant to suggest I was being punished by staying with them; unfortunately, I didn't get it. Instead, I sat at the table and nibbled at the bread and tried to act like it was okay—hoping to avoid being rude. Soon they all laughed and told me it was a joke, but I felt humiliated. I wound up crying all night.

During these stays, I realized instinctively that if I wanted attention from these strangers I'd have to go back to my habit of using theatricality to get it. By the time I was six, I'd learned to do the Charleston and sing *Ain't She Sweet?* and performed at the slightest pretext. I soon expanded this into a full-blown skit with comic bits added, among them a turn as a rich British woman and saying "la-ti-da" with a lot of posing, using whatever material I could find that would work as a boa. By the time I was seven, my repertoire included a bit that my father had taught me, imitating Lady Bird Johnson with a thick Texas accent: *"I cherish the beautiful countryside of this wonderful country. As I drive through the byways and highways, if I see a candy wrapper on the side of the road... (dramatically)... I stop... (choking back tears), and I pick... it... up.... (punchline) Lyndon saves candy wrappers."*

These were desperate acts of a little girl seeking attention, and they got results, so I persisted. I soon launched into imitations—doing a "camel walk" in a send up of my Mom's "Aunt Kissy." This was a slow, contorted walk enhanced by appropriate facial expressions. That tended to wow even the most jaded Altus audience.

By the time I was ten, I'd added a carefully observed and highly precise chicken walk, and got very adept at barnyard sounds: goats, cows, chickens and hogs. I was so accomplished that I eventually I won a trophy in a hog calling contest. My skills have not diminished since then—just a few years ago at the Los Angeles County fair, we wandered into the big hog house, where all the hogs were lying around, unusually quiet. I let out a long, powerful hog call, which ignited such noise and excitement among them that we had to flee.

It is said that a blind man's sense of hearing becomes more acute because he is forced, through misfortune, to rely on it more. I suppose in that way my theatrical impulse became highly developed at an early age to compensate for the loss of affection and attention most children got from their home life.

And then there were occasions when I got attention from adults when I wasn't seeking it. When I was seven I cut my sister's hair in the "layered" style popular then. Unfortunately, at the unveiling, my layers resembled tiers, like a Mayan pyramid. It was the first and last time I ever cut anyone's hair. Another dubious activity involved dressing up any dogs and cats in the vicinity in doll clothes, despite their vocal protests.

Perhaps the most productive activity we engaged in was playing Monopoly. In fact, playing games of many kinds proved my salvation in times like these, not only because they passed the time, but also because they connected me with my father. He had been an only child, and learned early on to entertain himself with made up games, and I definitely picked that up from him.

Many of the games he invented had a mathematical component. Have you ever been bored waiting in line at a bank or a store? Not us! My father would get out his watch and we'd count how many people would be served in how many minutes. Then we'd multiply by the number of people in front of us and make predictions about how long it would take for us to arrive at the front. Eventually we'd keep track over several visits and try to beat our old record. We did the same for cars traveling through signal lights. We also had a game for counting cars on a passing train, and card tricks involving counting.

I have no doubt that these games sparked my lifelong interest in puzzles and mathematics, which in turn would give rise to *The Grocery Game*.

When my mother was ill, she was usually hospitalized. But when she was well, she was full of vivacity and love, a free spirit unconcerned with trivialities, passionate about getting the most out of every moment she was alive

Instead of doing housework, she'd take us to the park or zoo. She was content to endure a less than perfect house in exchange for more moments of joy with her daughters in the brisk outdoors. When she did work on the house, she was very creative. She'd also remodel the kitchen in eccentric ways; one year, it was red, white and blue, another, hot pink.

When she did remodeling, she would often paint in the nude. I don't mean paint artwork; I mean the hallways and bedrooms. My sister and I would come home once in a while from school and find her occupied and attired thus, and her explanation was simple: any clothes she wore would be ruined by the paint, but if she had no clothing on, she was just a bath or shower away from being paint-free. On one occasion, my sister took a brush and painted my mother's bare butt, doubtless to help her test her theory.

She had a dozen wigs of different colors and styles, so we never knew who would greet us at home or at school. She loved play-acting—perhaps that's why it came so easily to me. Growing up, she had been a cheerleader, drum majorette and lead baton twirler, so like me, performing was in her blood.

My mother had a pet phrase—"I know *just* the thing!"— delivered in her endearing South Carolina twang—which she'd utter just before telling us a solution to some perplexing problem. Often she really *did* have good ideas. But sometimes her solutions were wacky, reminiscent of *I Love Lucy*.

On one such occasion, my father picked up chiggers—tiny bloodsucking insects—in his pants. My mother knew *just the thing:* apply nail polish to the bites, so as to seal off and suffocate the chiggers. Well, the application of this cure went smoothly, and it's quite possible that the chiggers suffered as my mother predicted. The problem arose in *removing* the nail polish a few days later—she used nail polish remover, which (it turns out) is rather harsh on certain sensitive parts of a man's anatomy. My father was literally screaming in pain. Subsequently, I think he preferred to take his chances with the chiggers. And after a while it got to be a running joke in our family— when she said "I know *just the thing*," run the other way!

My mother's upbringing in South Carolina profoundly affected one aspect of her values. She was raised by her grandmother, with the help of an African American nanny. My mother spoke about how odd she found it that her "Mammy" was so much part of the family, and yet was not allowed to eat with the family if guests were there. The injustice affected my mother deeply, and she had us read books by African American authors to help ensure we had respect for people of all races. "Black Like Me" by John Howard Griffin was the most profound, guaranteed to be life changing for anyone who ever thought racism in any way would be tolerable. Yet, I'm stunned by how few people have read it.

When I was eight, California reached her long arms out to us and drew us to her shores for a visit. When I was ten, she plucked us completely from Altus and we settled there. The occasion was a small church in Anaheim that needed a pastor, and a church in Altus whose pastor wanted a new challenge.

I had of course spent half my life in Altus, and had deep connections there, but when my father got the letter confirming that he'd been offered the position at the First Baptist Church in Anaheim, any hint of sentimentality left me. It felt like Christmas morning. We were under strict orders not to let anyone know until it was officially announced on Sunday, but I couldn't contain my excitement and told a friend of mine Sunday morning. Word spread like wildfire, and my father, who had given much thought and tender care to the words he would deliver announcing his departure, and wondered what the response of his flock might be, unexpectedly faced a standing ovation as he mounted the pulpit. I shrunk as far down in my pew as I could, but the waves of joy emanating from the congregation eased my feelings of guilt.

Considering how much of my life I'd spent in Altus, the days leading up to our departure were anti-climactic. I said goodbye to lifelong friends without realizing the significance of saying goodbye, not thinking that the love I had for them was fragile and would not— could not— survive the miles that would soon separate us. I gathered my things and packed them and re-packed them, counting down the hours till we climbed into the station wagon one last time. I spent the last weekend with my close friend Debra, who lived out side of town on a ranch, for one final picnic by the watering pond where the cattle would gather, as was our habit.

And then we were loaded onto the station wagon, with another car in tow, pulling out of our driveway. My father had a rule that we were not allowed to ask how far we had to go till we were out of sight of the house, so my sister and I sat in the back, facing the rear, and waited till the right moment before shouting out "How much further is it?" in unison at the top of our lungs.

It was the last time I ever saw our house in Altus.

19

On that last trip to California, as we raced across the southwestern desert in predawn darkness, I remember being the only one awake on the bus besides my father. I remember looking out the window, melodies drifting in and out of my mind, the landscape lit up by the full moon, and thought about how empty it was, how little there was, and how God had made something beautiful of it.

At that time, my attention was facing forward and I gave scant thought to Altus. But now, from a distance of many years, I marvel at how my mother and father had likewise made so much from so little, always bringing their imagination, humor and love to our lives.

Altus is for me the place where there was a fight every Saturday night—a *food* fight, around the dinner table—and my parents would join in and everyone would help clean up afterward.

Altus is where standing in a boring bank line became an exciting spectator sport.

Altus is where, for one Halloween party, my father dressed in drag—with makeup and one of my mother's dresses—and my mother became too ill to attend, so he went without her, and was pestered by a strange skinny man in galoshes with a stocking mask on his face, who showed up uninvited—and who later proved to be my mother, likewise dressed in drag, giving to him as good as she got.

Altus is where my father, treated to a big dinner at a churchgoer's home, heaped his plate high with his favorite food— buttered potatoes—only to discover they were buttered turnips—which he hated—and after he ate them anyway he was treated to big piles of buttered turnips whenever he visited any churchgoer's house. And it's where my mother one night served him up a big pile of buttered turnips, disguised as potatoes—just to get a rise out of him.

But most of all Altus is the place where my mother's love of her daughters and of life overcame severe illness, where my father's love of God and music traveled far and wide from a small speck on the map of Oklahoma, and where I was given the gifts of music, of performance, of play, and was able to share them on journeys westward.

3. Orange

Orange County was full of promise when we arrived shortly after my tenth birthday in 1970. It was a booming suburban utopia, with farmers and orange groves rapidly being uprooted and replaced by young families and tract houses, where Disneyland, just fifteen years old, remained a one-of-a-kind destination and somehow had more magic than it does now, where Major League Baseball had recently arrived in the form of the California Angels.

We bought a simple one story house in the city of Orange, not far from my father's church in Anaheim. The house was small, and the church was not much bigger. Its congregation could barely support us, so we lived modestly indeed.

The latest fashions that beckoned to me from commercials, clothes racks, and classmates were too expensive, so I improvised a way of getting them without the money: with my mother's help, I learned to design and sew my own clothes.

I remember one episode early in learning the ropes, so to speak, of sewing. I was home alone (my mother working at the church office), and while I was working on a dress I wanted to wear to church the next day, the sewing machine came un-threaded. I was very frustrated, but fortunately I was able to have my mother talk me through re-threading over the phone. I was able to finish the dress in time, but I didn't know how to do the facing around the neckline, so it was a bit rumply.

A number of ladies at church approached me and said with transparent mockery, "What a pretty dress. Did your mommy make it for you?"

"No—*I* did!" I snapped. I knew that it didn't look quite right, but I was still proud of it. Quickly, their snide attitude turned to amazement that a ten-year-old could make a dress that well.

From those humble beginnings, my skills developed so much that by middle school I was often the most fashionably attired student in class. In this, I was surely following in the tradition of my Grand-Daddy in seeing patterns in things where others did not, and making them come alive by the work of my own hands.

Other pleasures of Southern California were not expensive— the warm sunshine, the playgrounds, and the beaches, which were only a twenty minute drive from my home.

Soon after we settled in Southern California, my parents decided it was time to expand our family by one child—something they'd long planned to do. When my mother got pregnant, in late 1969, we were ecstatic, and the church threw us a huge baby shower.

Unfortunately, on June 6, 1970, my baby sister, Lynda Michelle, was still-born. We were devastated. I remember my mother disappearing for hours at a time during the months that followed, and I later learned she was mourning at the baby's gravesite. We all searched for the meaning of the loss; it was a particularly trying time for my father, a man of God who felt betrayed.

Eventually, we did find meaning in the tragedy, as best we could discern it: my parents decided to adopt a baby. After several fruitless months, our family doctor called and told us of woman who was due to deliver a child that December, who wanted us to have it.

That Christmas morning, we got the call, and my baby brother Jimmy arrived in our house two days later. He was instantly an integral part of our family, each of us loving him just as we loved each other.

Unfortunately, my mother continued to have periodic bouts of pancreatitis, and each time she suffered, we suffered too. Her long hospital stays had taught us all too well what life was like without her, and with each bout there lingered a fear the loss would be permanent.

Because of my mother's illness, I started to do the family grocery shopping around age thirteen; sometimes I put my baby brother in the a stroller and walked into town to the local supermarket. Usually, I was given ten or twenty dollars to get some essentials, like eggs or milk, and maybe a few other specific items.

My frugal nature—something I likely learned from my father, product of the Dust Bowl—kicked in. I started noticing a huge difference in prices on various brands of things like peanut butter, hot dogs and cereal. By shopping wisely, I was able to come home with more than I was asked for in most cases. I looked for sales, and started realizing that I had seen coupons for some of those things that we bought, so I started cutting coupons and bringing them with me. I figured out that if I could wait until some of these coupon items went on sale, I could buy them for very little.

Now, when I was sent to the store with ten dollars for eggs, cheese and milk, I would spend a little more time checking my coupons against sales. I remember my brother would get tired of these long grocery store trips. To me it was a game, but to him it was a boring ordeal. So I turned that problem into a game: if I planned on buying a box of cereal, I would grab that first, and put a pile on his little stroller tray. He would be happy for a while, until the sugar kicked in, and then he would try to get out of the stroller to climb the shelves. I had to adapt to this small window of opportunity to play my game and win.

Most of the time, my mother was well, and by the time I was a teenager, we'd become very close. In some ways this prevented me from developing close relationships with my peers. I didn't really know how to develop friendships with girls my age. My mother was my best friend, and that had advantages over a normal peer relationship. 'Her free-spirit style persisted while we were in California; on many occasions when I was in school I'd get called down the office, where I found my mother waiting to take me to a doctor's appointment—which promptly proved to be a visit to the beach, or shopping, or on one occasion to Little Tokyo near downtown Los Angeles to try this exotic dish called *sushi*.

On another occasion, she took me to Olvera Street in downtown Los Angeles, a historic area featuring Mexican shops and restaurants.

We were jaywalking across Alameda Street when a foot patrol officer blew his whistle and signaled for us to stop. He strode up to us.

"Gotta stay within the crosswalk," he said as he got out his ticket book.

"The what?" my mother said, pouring on her lilting accent.

"The crosswalk, the crosswalk, you've never heard of a crosswalks?" the officer said without looking up.

"Why, no" my mother said. "Whatever is it for?"

I held my breath, assuming we would both soon be in big trouble, but my mother *knew just the thing.*

The officer looked at her. "You've got to walk within the crosswalk. That thing there." He pointed derisively.

"You mean those little lines are just for little ole me to cross the street?" my mother lilted. "Why how cle-a-vah."

Now I was *sure* we'd wind up in the slammer. But instead, the officer laughed. "Where are you from, ma'am?"

"Holly Hill, South Carolina. And let me tell you, folks in Holly Hill would *love* to have one of those there crosswalks. Little ole folks are crossing streets all the time and have no place whatever in which to cross. When I get back the first thing I'm going to do is suggest that they put a crosswalk in, maybe two or three, so people will have little ole lines in which to walk whenever and wherever they need to cross. I don't know how to thank you telling us all about this, which I will gladly share with all the folks back home."

By this time the officer was laughing heartily. "You're quite welcome, ma'am; have a good visit." He put away his ticket book and walked away.

We made it safely around a corner before breaking into laughter

But my acute awareness of my mother's fragility sometimes colored even the most joyful times. Her attacks always occurred unexpectedly, always accompanied by the fear that she'd be taken from us against our will and hope.

One way I coped with my anxiety was to bury myself in my schoolwork. I found the curriculum of California public schools was behind that which we'd known in Oklahoma, and I got the reputation of being the smart kid. Good grades came easily to me. I did so well, in fact, that Portola Junior High built a separate room for me in seventh grade—a room with padded walls, no less.

It wasn't *strictly* for me, but I was the first to use it. It was a sound-proof testing room, where select "lucky" students were chosen to take a series of tests for a program called MGM.—"Mentally Gifted Minors." For three weeks I spent much time in there taking a battery of tests from standard I.Q. to "photographic memory" tests. If it turned out you had photographic memory, they'd give you further exercises to help you develop it.

As a consequence of my performance, I was advised to skip eighth grade altogether, and was given a book called *50 Days to a More Powerful Vocabulary* in order to compensate for my lost class time. A book in exchange for a year of schooling? I wasn't sure if it was because these school officials thought so much of me, or so little of eighth grade.

Thus, with some misgivings, but with my parents' encouragement, I entered ninth grade in the fall of my thirteenth year. It may have been a wise choice academically, but personally it was a disaster. I lost whatever friendships I'd cultivated for the three years since arriving in California, and I was an unknown entity to my new classmates in ninth grade, who, once they discovered my story, resented me for being a geek who was allowed to skip eighth grade.

By the middle of that academic year, I had made scant headway into re-establishing my social presence in school. I was anxious about the school work, anxious about friends, and anxious about all manner of teenage concerns.

On the night of December 28, 1973, these various anxieties were put immediately into perspective by the sound of someone banging cupboards in the kitchen.

I was asleep in the front bedroom of the house, isolated from the others, whose bedrooms were in the back. I was awakened by that odd sound, and I figured it was my father making too much noise seeking a midnight snack. I ignored it but was soon stirred by the hollering of my mother—desperate to wake me up. I rolled out of bed, disoriented, and stumbled to the door.

As soon as I flung it open, I was hit by a blast of heat and smoke. The banging I heard was the sound of drywall cracking and support timbers breaking in a raging fire. I slammed the door shut and began to pray.

To the rear of the house, my mother had likewise been awakened by the noise and discovered the house on fire. She in turn awakened my father, who proceeded to take a deep gulp of air before reopening the door and sprinting down the hallway to rouse my sister and baby brother. All had been spared death from smoke inhalation because their doors had been closed.

My mother and father got my sister and baby brother out of the house, but I was trapped. Even though I was on the first floor, and the window was an obvious choice, I was disoriented and the obvious did not occur to me. Instead, I took a deep breath of what remained of the fresh air in my room, then threw open the door and made my way through the hallway to the front entrance. I know I was going as fast as I could, but I can remember the scene as if played out in slow motion, with flames all around me and burning timbers falling down on either side. I felt I'd seen this before, and in a way I had: it seemed like the *Pirates of the Caribbean* ride at Disneyland.

I made it out safely into the chill of the night, and found my mother, sister and baby brother gathered out front, along with some neighbors, their faces lit by flames that now arched up as high as the telephone poles.

My father was not among us, and instantly I was sure he was dead. My mother got down on her knees and prayed for him. Some neighbors drew close to comfort her. Soon enough, a large explosion came from inside the house, and we could see timbers shifting and a big burst of sparks and flame rising even higher in the sky. The sight confirmed our worst fears.

As we contemplated this tragedy, my father came running toward us from around the side of the house, unnerved but otherwise unhurt. He had remained behind trying to make sure everyone was clear.

As we gazed in shock at the flaming ruins, my father repeatedly counted us to make sure we were all there. Our car, a Ford LTD, was parked in the driveway right next to the garage, and the flames were getting close. We expected a climactic pyrotechnical display would erupt soon.

"Want to save your car?" a teenage kid asked my father as we all stared.

"I can't," he replied, frustrated. "I don't have the keys."

The teenager nodded. "I'll get it for you, if you'd like."

"I told you," my father said, growing impatient. "I don't have the keys."

"Do you want me to get it for you or not?" asked the kid, persisting.

"How are you going to get it?"

"Just tell me one way or another."

"Yes," my father said at last, exasperated.

As the gathering crowd watched, the boy sprinted to the car, opened its hood, and in no time hotwired it. He managed to back the car out the driveway without use of the steering wheel, which was locked.

Thanks to that resourceful teenage boy, our car was spared. We'd lost just about everything else, but at least could get still around.

By now the fire trucks had arrived, along with medics. A medic examined me and discovered that though I was unhurt, my fingernail polish had bubbled from the heat during my brief run through the hallway. She showed my hand to another medic, and the two marveled.

"What's wrong?" I asked.

"You're lucky," she said. "The heat was so intense it tore through the acetone. I've seen this before—but only on dead people."

As the firefighters watered down the flaming embers, I knew we had survived with what was important. But the cold December breeze, blowing against my thin night gown, reminded me how little else we had left. All the clothing and accessories I'd made—so important to my fragile self-esteem, were gone. Our whole family would be living on donated clothing for a while.

Afterwards, I marveled at how God had taken care of us by having us close all the doors as we went to sleep, an action we rarely ever took, especially with an infant in the house. But it also occurred to me that if God had been looking out for us, why had he allowed the fire in the first place? I was a child, and could come up with no satisfactory answer to that question—and as an adult, I still cannot. I do know that the experience shifted my values: after fire, I could never sympathize with my friends' obsession with acquiring "things." I lost interest in material stuff.

In the months that followed—the unhappy spring of ninth grade, rendered unhappier still by the fire—we stayed in various motels and in the houses of members of my father's congregation. It was just like old times when my sister and I used to stay in strangers' houses, except that now we had company—my parents and baby brother. As a coup de grace to my misbegotten and thoroughly dreary ninth grade, when we moved at last into a new house, it was in neighboring Anaheim.

As a sophomore, I'd be starting over at a new school in a new city.

4. Making It Work

"No!" I cried before my mother had even finished reading aloud the letter I received from an advanced education specialist at Loara High's Mentally Gifted Minors program. "I am *not* going to be a geek this time! I am *not* going to be different!"

I arrived fresh and optimistic at Loara High in the fall of 1974, ready to start life anew. Unfortunately, my storied academic past followed me, and whetted the appetite of the school's administrators, who received a modest amount of extra money from the state for each student enrolled in their gifted children program.

Within a few days of the start of school, I was given a note by my homeroom teacher to report to the principal's office, where the advanced education specialist, a small lady with glasses and very tight hair greeted me with an overly gracious smile. She sat me down in her office and told me that given my academic record, I was wasting my time with conventional schoolwork—not *challenged* enough—and that I'd be better off enrolling in their Mentally Gifted Minors program. She went on to tell me about all the advantages: I'd be eligible to test out of normal classes and skip them, and then take more advanced classes and participate in special field trips and social gatherings. She assured me I'd be much happier.

I listened to her patiently, then politely declined and got up to leave. She was shocked. She persisted for several weeks afterward, and finally wrote a letter to my parents, extolling the program.

"This is the first chance I have just to be a normal person," I told my mother. "I actually have a chance to have friends and not be so hated by everybody."

My father picked up and examined the letter, and agreed with me. If I wanted to be a normal teen, a normal teen is what I was entitled to be.

Thus I successfully fought off a second attempt by school officials to use my academic success to derail my life. It was not the last time I would deal with the pressure to be different, but avoiding the MGM program gave me a much-needed reprieve. By this time, my earlier endeavors in designing my own clothes had blossomed into a full-blown interest in beauty and fashion. By eleventh grade, I was still singing in the church choir, but was also, with my mother's encouragement, getting work as a fashion model, and going out on commercial auditions.

To some extent, my mother's encouragement reflected her own frustrations of having nowhere to express her love of performing in the remoteness of Enid, Oklahoma, where she spent her teenage years. She could dream bigger dreams for me, though, and when we settled in Orange—a mere thirty-five miles from Hollywood—she took immediate advantage. Within a few months, she entered me in the Little Miss America beauty contest at the Hollywood Palladium. Unfortunately, I had already hit a growth spurt, rendering me ungainly, while my competition consisted of cute little girls as yet untouched by the onslaught of adolescence. It was an unsuccessful, not to mention tedious, outing, but it was just a start.

By the time I was sixteen, the ungainliness of early adolescence was behind me, and I signed with a modeling agency, Mary Webb Davis. Soon thereafter, I went on to Hollywood agents and managers specializing in actors, and my mother didn't need to encourage me at all anymore; I got the bug, and was loving it, and she was there to cheer me on. She also would sometimes stay up late into the night, sewing just the perfect dress for a photo shoot or audition.

I was able to drive myself up to Los Angeles for auditions and photo shoots several times a month—no mean feat for an inexperienced driver. One problem in particular vexed my mother, though—after one photo shoot, I came home after dark. She did not like me driving through rougher parts of Los Angeles at night. But she knew *just the thing*—she immediately went to Goodwill and bought me a man's hat. After that, I'd put my hair up into it when driving alone after dark—adopting a role I'd never played in my years on stage—a young guy.

As for the photo shoots themselves, I was a natural. I had a long history of hamming it up for the camera dating to my childhood, so when professional photographers started asking me to work with the camera, I felt like I was finally given the opportunity to shine. But more than that, I was motivated by the money: I made $150 an hour, with a three hour minimum.

The long hair that I so studiously hid under a hat while driving paid dividends for me early in my modeling career. I won a contest for *Long and Silky* hair products and got money and lots of gifts. Later, I landed a print ad for *Seventeen* Magazine for the shampoo line *Gee Your Hair Smells Terrific*. The photo featured me in a swing under a big, beautiful tree in a Beverly Hills park, with a good looking male model pushing me. I had a three hour minimum, so even though it took not quite an hour, I made $450 for having fun on a swing! I was on cloud nine.

The key to enjoying the experience was that I didn't take it too seriously, though in that I was something of a rarity. In fact, the audition process gave me an early exposure to one of the more unsavory aspects of the entertainment industry: cutthroat competition. At one modeling audition, I made the mistake of leaving my portfolio, containing the standard 11x14" photos, sitting on a waiting room chair when I went into the ladies' room. When I came out, my portfolio was nowhere to be found. I was in a panic, and the other models in the room did their best to hide their faces.

Finally, one girl piped up and said that it was behind the potted palm. A girl who was then in the office interviewing had hidden it from me before she got called in. I saw her come out of the door, and I had my portfolio in my lap. She looked guilty. And she also looked a lot like me.

Too much competition for her, I suppose.

I got the job. It was a billboard and commercial for a clothing store chain called County Seat, and within months life-size posters of me in the jeans were gracing the walls of its many stores throughout the southern United States.

As eleventh grade progressed, I found that my popularity had zoomed, and I felt the promise Southern California offered to me when I arrived as a ten year old was at last being fulfilled.

Reflecting back on it, it's unfortunate I felt the need to put my academic abilities under wraps for fear of being different. Yet despite my lack of interest things academic, I still had no trouble earning straight-*A*'s. For this, I received as punishment still more attention from the advanced education specialist, who redoubled her efforts to enroll me in MGM. In an act of defiance, I deliberately sabotaged myself in Chemistry during the fall semester, earning the first and only C of my entire school career. The course itself was not hard; I simply refused to do some of the work. It's noteworthy thinking back on it that I did not opt for an *F.* My objective was to be average, to blend in, and an *F* would have made me stand out, on the opposite end of the academic spectrum.

But even in "dumbing down," I found that the influence of my father—in particular, his infectious love of math puzzles and games— asserted itself in both positive and negative ways. On the positive side, it led me to a keen interest in computer science, in the days when the word *computer* did not indicate a keyboard, monitor and mouse but rather a room-sized machine with punch cards. I would input data and do statistics on earned run averages for the high school baseball team and have them printed in the school newspaper.

On the negative side, during my course of study, I developed, along with a few friends, a keen interest in the chemical interactions involved in creating contact explosives. Our experiments proved to be an overwhelming success as we proceeded to test our "theories" in the high school parking lot after school one fall day. We successfully blew up a several beer bottles, a shoebox and a trash can.

When the police arrived, I was surprised to find myself under threat of custody, and quite fearful of my parents' reaction when they got my phone call from the jailhouse. Fortunately, we were treated quite leniently—a warning—and I ascribed this initially to my reputation as a good student and not a troublemaking rebel. It was half true. The real author of the leniency was none other than the advanced education specialist, who had interceded on our behalf.

By now my own sense of guilt became her chief weapon, and at last I agreed to enroll in MGM, on one condition: I not be required to attend these additional classes or social gatherings; I would simply do the work. She agreed: as long as I continued to get *A*'s, she was willing to sign documents stating I'd attended these activities when I hadn't. The school got its extra money, and I avoided being an intellectual castoff.

In a sense, I have to thank the advanced education specialist for more than getting me out of high school without a police record: she also allowed me to live a charmed life of a Southern California teen. Now unencumbered by the need to sit in a classroom, I began to spend a considerable amount of time on school days down at Huntington Beach, and my chief occupation there was lying in the sand and "looking pretty," which was not as easy as it sounds. There was always a temptation to fall asleep on the beach blanket in the warm sun and refreshing breeze, but if you fell asleep there was a good chance you'd wake up with drool on your face, and that definitely *wasn't* pretty.

Soon enough I worked out a routine with my sister Karen, also a straight-*A* student with a similar skill for ditching classes on a sunny day: we'd take turns, one of us sleeping while the other kept an eye out for cute guys. The moment we had an imminent sighting, the one on watch would say, "Wake up; you're ugly!" or a similar warning. So it may seem that lying on the beach on a sunny school day was not a lot of hard work… but, well, it's not.

And inevitably there were glitches that would arise in our system. There was one occasion when Karen had just undergone oral surgery and her mouth was still numb. When a group of guys I knew from school were approaching (Huntington Beach is often populated with teenagers on school days—the Pacific Ocean is a magnet that draws them irresistibly from high school classrooms), I told her to just smile and not talk, because her speech would be slurred from the anesthetic.

I carried the conversation with the guys, and it began well enough as we exchanged views about school, teachers, mutual friends, and who was seen going out with who, and through it all Karen duly smiled and nodded.

Soon enough, though, the guys stopped smiling and there were some awkward pauses, because they weren't helping much with the conversation.

Finally one said, "Well, gotta go," and they waved and walked away.

Karen turned to me with drool running out of her mouth and said, "That was weird."

Weird indeed!

It may seem that I was living a very self-indulgent life for daughter of a Baptist minister, I still helped minister to the poor occasionally, but these endeavors became far less frequent. In my senior year, I came up with an innovative way engage in charitable activity again.

One evening early that fall, my boyfriend came over to our house, quite distraught. He had a history paper due the next day, and hadn't even started. I looked over his assignment, which was modest, and his notes, which were slender indeed, and offered to help him. As the evening wore on, I realized it was much easier for me to simply write it than for me to help *him* write it. I told him to go home and relax, and the next morning I handed him his paper, neatly typed.

A week later he got his paper back and earned an *A* on it, and I was very proud of him, and he, of me. And the teacher was proud of me as well: he scribbled "Good work, Teri," at the bottom. I'm not sure how he knew it was my handiwork; perhaps he recognized my style from a class I took with him the year before. In any event, word spread quickly among the students about my talent with research papers, and soon three of his friends asked me to help them with *their* papers.

As much as I liked his friends, I felt it was wrong to do their work for them, while they got off scot-free. At the same time, I felt it was also wrong to miss an opportunity to help my fellow man. So I came quickly to a simple formulation: An *A* would cost them fifty dollars, a *B* forty and a *C* thirty.

Within a month I was doing a brisk business in all kinds of papers, often sketching out abstracts while at the beach, then typing them up when I got home. I got so good that even when contracted for a *B* or *C,* I wound up getting my clients *A*'s. I suppose it wasn't, ultimately, the most honorable thing to do, but I rationalized it thus: as long as the school district was earning extra money off of my intellect, why shouldn't I do the same thing?

During my high school years, I did not neglect my athletic side. I used to run in Anaheim, with a classmate who always seemed to be several steps ahead in any race: Mary Decker, who later blossomed to international fame. But my real athletic love had a more violent aspect: In my junior year in high school, and until I got married in 1980. I was heavily into Kung Fu martial arts.

It began when some of the guys I knew began talking about an amazing Kung Fu teacher named Wally Soto. Wally had an unusual studio for two reasons: one, it was in his garage. And two: it was illegal.

Wally was a disciple of the old Bruce Lee style. He didn't train on rubber mats; he used a concrete floor, slick with dancing wax. To stand in a "horse stance" with your feet slipping apart was killer, and would make you sweat within a few minutes.

Wally would say, "If you ever got into a rumble, what were you going to do? Say 'Pardon me, while I go and get my rubber mat'?

It was illegal to not have rubber mats—no insurance company would cover his business—so it was "underground," and I'm sure that appealed to me. Certainly it was consistent with the subversive, rebellious aspects of my life—ditching classes and cheating for friends on papers.

Unfortunately, Wally only worked with guys. I came to watch a few times, and got one of the guys to talk to him for me to ask if I could train with him. He said 'no,' but this was a time for me of pushing limits, and I did so with Wally. I implored him to give me six months, and if I couldn't beat someone at a brown belt level (an intermediate rank) by then, he'd never hear from me again. He agreed.

Six months of intense workouts later, I scored very highly in beating a brown belt at a tournament, and wound up working out with Wally four or five times a week for the next five years.

Wally always told us that if we got in a rumble, "You will break bones," though he always told us to try to avoid rumbles at all costs.

Which I did.

Until the spring of 1980.

I had just left my Kung Fu workout, and decided I was too thirsty to make it home without something to drink. When I spotted a 7-11, I pulled over to get a Coke. I was still wearing my Kung Fu T-shirt, with a wrap around skirt. I was also wearing high heels—fortunately, they were easy to slip off, as I would soon discover.

As I got out of my car, I heard several male voices shouting out very vulgar words. I looked and saw three guys in a Mustang, whooping and hollering, and looking like they'd already had a few beers. And suddenly I realized they were addressing their foul language at me.

I ignored them and headed for the store entrance, when one got out of the car. He was over six feet tall and about 200 pounds, and had a nasty attitude as he strolled up to me.

"Whore!"

I slipped off my high heels, with the intent to make a run for it, but he got to me very quickly and soon was within arm's reach. As he reached out toward me, finely-tuned reactions I'd honed for four years took over me.

I blocked his arm with a right back knuckle roundhouse sweep.

That was probably enough to get him to leave me alone.

But without hesitating or thinking, I followed with a left back knuckle roundhouse (making contact with his face), an overhead right hanging punch (making contact with his head), and another right back knuckle that sweeps back down, and simultaneously, with my left, I reached out to pull him back in by his hair (as he was falling backwards) to pull him into a right front snap kick, which is intended for the solar plexus, to knock the wind out of an assailant.

Unfortunately, though, I got a little over-amped, and either jerked him too far forward, or kicked too high. In any event, I got him in the mouth, and left him in a heap.

I was shaking, but trying to remain cool.

I slipped back on my high heels, and headed into the 7-11 to get what I came for. It had happened so quickly that I still had my left hand in a tight fist, and when I reached to open the refrigerator door in the 7-11, a wad of his hair fell out of my opened fist. That just gave me the heebie-jeebies.

I bought my Coke, went out to my car, and tried not to look, but I could see that they had put the big guy in the front passenger seat of the Mustang.

I got into my car quickly and locked the doors as a friend of his walked over to me. I probably would have pulled out immediately, but I noticed he was laughing quietly to himself. He leaned into my window, which I opened a crack.

"I think you broke his ribs."

"No way," I said, recalling the moves I'd made. I didn't remember kicking him in the ribs. Of course, it had all happened so fast, perhaps I was wrong.

"He also bit his tongue," the guy said.

I glanced over and saw my assailant literally soaked in blood, which stained the front of his white t-shirt. I could also hear him groaning loudly.

"Too bad," I said. "He deserved it."

"He did," the guy agreed.

"You'd better take him to the hospital," I said.

After I drove off and calmed down, I felt bad about what I'd done. I'd intended to disable him—prevent him from hurting me—but I did not want to do any permanent damage or scar him. I was also worried they'd track me down and sue me, or stick me with his medical bills or something.

Curiously, about two years later, a guy came up to me, kind of chuckling, and identified me as "the chick who beat up my friend." I was cagey about it, not willing to admit the truth. We argued back and forth, and soon enough he realized I wouldn't cop to it. So he assured me that I had nothing to worry about in terms of repercussions: true enough, the guy went to the hospital and did have three broken ribs and a bitten tongue. But he didn't admit a slender, 125 pound blonde female had done the damage; he claimed he'd been assaulted by three guys with baseball bats.

Wally had, in five years' time, given me defensive firepower equivalent to three gangbangers.

I'd like to say I'm not proud of what happened, but I guess deep down inside, I do feel proud that I had the ability to defend myself. Ultimately, I really don't know if he would have hurt me, but I didn't wait to find out.

Something else occurs to me now, thinking back on it: the fact that I had prepared so carefully and thoroughly for this decisive moment. So much of my life to that point had been dedicated to careful preparation, from the extensive planning and fundraising for our trips out west from Altus, to my many appearances onstage in my father's shows, which were extensively rehearsed; even the performances I gave as a lonely child in the houses of strangers required preparation: memorization and rehearsal of various routines. This habit of mine, in the form of five years of martial arts workouts—had spared me potential disaster at the 7-11, and in later years, the careful preparation that went into the procedure I adopted in shopping eventually became The Grocery Game

It's possible that the life I'd created for myself in high school was *too* complete. The system was so refined and carefully balanced that it was perhaps subject to being upset easily. Or it's possible that in its intricacies there were contradictions that threatened to pull it apart without my realizing it. I was earning straight *A*'s in a gifted children's program in which my chief class consisted of sunning myself at Huntington Beach; I was writing *A* papers for dozens of classmates while being crowned Miss Teen Anaheim in 1976; I made $150 a week using my brain on research papers and $150 an hour using my face in fashion photo shoots.

In another culture there may not have been any contradiction at all in a woman using both brains and beauty to get ahead, but in

43

America in the late twentieth century, the cultural assumption was that the two were mutually exclusive: a woman has to choose.

Upon graduation from Anaheim High in 1977, I chose beauty. It wasn't a momentous choice, made all at once, but a choice arrived at by default, piece by piece. I enrolled without much enthusiasm in Cypress Junior College in the fall of that year, while seeing high school classmates not as accomplished as I was—including some whose grade point averages benefited from my hard work on their research papers—move on to more prestigious four year colleges.

Meanwhile I was getting regular photo and commercial work. The instant gratification of earning money doing modeling pulled me away from academics. On top of that, my mother developed a severe case of pancreatitis in November and ended up in the intensive care unit again fighting for her life.

I suppose I intended to go back to school in the spring semester, but never did, and aside from sporadic attempts to re-enroll over the next few years, my formal education was effectively over. As to more prestigious four year colleges to which my friends migrated, I never gave them serious thought. I had no money, and scholarships did not occur to me. Besides, the Junior college was local, and that gave me the luxury of flexibility—I could better deal with unexpected opportunities—like auditions or photo shoots—and unwelcome crises, like tending to my mother during bouts of illness

Ultimately, though, I did fail to fulfill my academic promise, and have, ever since, felt a twinge of inferiority to those who hold degrees.

Why didn't I ever pick up that thread of my life again and pursue higher learning? My father held a Masters degree, though it is worth noting that my mother never went beyond high school. Thinking back on it, it occurs to me that not once in my life did my parents mention the possibility of my going on to college, or prepare me for it. Perhaps it was just in their mindset—girls didn't go to college; boys did. Perhaps it was also the fact that our family was wracked by the chronic crisis of my mother's health, and this, combined with the constant need to make ends meet on a modest minister's income, made short-term thinking dominate our mindset. When a loved one is sick, and bills must be paid, the future seems fraught with danger, not promise, so I adopted a more free-spirited approach to life, living for the day. I do know that if I had wanted to go on to college, my parents would have supported me wholeheartedly.

The full implications of withdrawing from school were not apparent to me at that time. Aside from my mother's illness, the world was full of promise for me. The pressure was on for me to make a living, and it was thrilling to do it in the glamour industry.

Even taking less-glamorous part-time jobs was part of an exciting new world of adulthood. At one of these, in which I worked as a dental assistant, I discovered how dysfunctional a marital relationship can be, and how the drive for money can lead to the risk of ruin.

The problem was not the dentist, a slight middle-aged man. He was diligent, well-trained, and board certified. He was polite to his patients and subordinates. The problem was sitting in his front office.

His wife.

While the dentist wore the simple white uniform of the dental profession, his wife wore furs even when it was hot. He wore a simple wedding band; her fingers were studded with jewel-encrusted rings, and other jewelry adorned every available location on her person. He was patient with his patients; she was not.

The wife lived way beyond his means, and saw it as her duty to be his motivator and bill collector. She answered his phones and never turned down a patient for an appointment, whether there was room on the schedule or not. In her spare moments, she would call and harass anyone late with paying a bill, and many who weren't late at all.

There were four rooms in the office, and we typically used only the front three. Just before ten one morning in late July 1978, a young man arrived unexpectedly for a ten o'clock teeth cleaning. The wife had overbooked us again, and the front three rooms were taken, so the dentist led him to the fourth room, put the suction tube in his mouth and told him the he'd be back shortly. He then placed the man's chart in the pocket outside the door.

The wife, unknown to the dentist or anyone else, promptly removed the chart in order to find out whether the young man was current in his accounts payable. Then she got distracted hounding another customer for money, and promptly forgot to replace the chart.

For the next two hours, the dentist and I dealt with wave after wave of patients, overbooked by the wife, and because the young man was in a seldom used room with the door only slightly ajar, we forgot about him.

When I took my lunch break, I noticed him sitting quietly and asked the dentist who he was.

"Oh my God," said the dentist, color draining from his face. We rushed to the room and found the young man asleep with the suction tube still in his mouth.

"You've got to wake him up and explain what happened," the dentist told me.

"I'm not doing that!" I replied.

The dentist gathered his strength, gently awakened the young man and removed the suction tube from his mouth. We were both all smiles as he looked at us.

"Sorry, we got a little busy; we'll get to you in just a moment," the dentist said.

"That's fine," the young man said, a little groggy. "But if I could please have a glass of water. I'm *very* thirsty."

I immediately sprang to work giving him water by the cupful while the dentist gave him a quick teeth cleaning and sent him on his way. It wasn't till he was practically out the door that he noticed the lateness of the hour, and even then he expressed no anger at us, just dismay over how late it was.

We'd gotten off lightly; the wife's hunger for money had nearly caused a disaster.

By making money through day jobs and modeling, I was pulling my own weight in the household, but I was helping in other ways as well. In my late teenage years, I started applying my aptitude with numbers and my love of games to the process of grocery shopping. I became an avid "couponer," and in carefully organizing and planning shopping trips, I was helping my family save a significant amount of money.

By the fall of 1979, I had adjusted to the adult working world; I had enlisted in acting lessons to further enhance my career path in acting, and had a vibrant social life; I was making headway in my modeling career, and ahead of me I saw nothing so daunting that my energy and ambition could not overcome. The vestiges of childhood were letting go of me with the exception of one bit of unfinished business: in November 1979, my mother took seriously ill. In her illness I felt again all the deepest and most profound fears of my early years. We all cared and prayed for her, and held day and night vigils at her bedside, but this time there would be no joyful homecoming.

47

After six anguished weeks, she passed away on December 28, 1979—six years to the day that our house burned to the ground.

My childhood was over.

5. Greg

Through most of history, those who have made a living in the dramatic arts—performers of various kinds, actors, singers, musicians, magicians, and their like—have made a slender living indeed. Shakespeare did well, but most of the itinerant laborers in the performing arts toiled anonymously and died impoverished. In the present day, though, there is a confluence of the performing arts and wealth—at least for those lucky enough to get a foot in the door of the entertainment industry—and as the seventies became the eighties, my life was taking me on a trajectory upward into that intersection.

If I can trace the origin of that trajectory, it would be to June 18, 1979, at a "cold reading" acting workshop in Hollywood. I'd been attending the workshop for a few months as part of my effort to expand my skills and horizons beyond Anaheim, and in it we studied how to perform a scene on the spot, from a script that had just been given to us.

June 18 promised to be similar to other nights I'd spent in the workshop, though I arrived there with some anticipation. An actress friend named Jill had been seeing this stunt man named Greg—and bragging about him for weeks, how handsome he was, and how great his buns were—exalting him to such a degree my friend Rita and I decided Jill had simply invented him. We told her to stop talking about him until she actually brought him in person.

On June 18, Jill delivered. Boy, did she deliver. In my view, Jill had understated her case for him. Greg was a *babe*.

I said a polite "hi" and shook his hand, then did my best to refocus my energy on the cold reading going on onstage. When the two actresses up there were through, the teacher, Steve, gave them a few notes, then called me up onstage and handed me a scene from the script of a movie called *Lifeguard*. He then peered into the audience for an actor to join me, but found none. Jill half-seriously offered up Greg for the part, and to her surprise Greg was willing, and to everyone's surprise, Steve was okay with it.

The scene we were to play involved two lovers.

Suddenly I was cast in the role of the lover of a guy I thought was gorgeous, and his girlfriend was the one responsible. The whole situation was straight out of Hollywood—and why not? It *was* Hollywood!

We both read through the scene quickly to ourselves, then, scripts in hand, launched into the scene, which began with an argument. I told him I was going to Marrakesh with another guy—a clumsy attempt to make him jealous. It worked, though; he immediately tried to woo me back, telling me he wanted to be "king of the jungle," but that as king he'd rule "gently." It was my turn to fall for it; we did a delicate verbal dance for a page or so before winding up on the couch, our faces close, our voices in a kind of "baby talk."

"Come on," I cooed. "Give me a *woof!*"

"*Woof!*"

"You my wittle teddy bear, what I wuvs," I said, one eye on the script and one eye on him.

"*Woof, woof!*"

We both looked down at the script. It said: "They make out passionately."

What could we do? We followed the script.

And that part I think I did convincingly, because I wasn't acting at all.

I didn't see the look on Jill's face at that point, but I imagine she, too, gave a very genuine performance of jealous rage from her spot in the audience.

After we received a few—mostly positive—notes from Steve, I shook hands with Greg and went down to the seats while Jill took her turn with Rita doing another scene on stage. The theater was mostly empty, and as I sat their catching my breath and watching my friends perform, I saw Greg re-enter the theater. He could have sat down anywhere, but made his way gradually to me, while my heart was pounding. At last he sat right next to me.

"You were very good," he said.

"I can't believe you've never acted," I told him.

"Who said I haven't?"

"I guess I don't know much about you," I said.

We sat a while, watching Rita and Jill massacre a scene from some obscure film.

"Want to get out of here?" he said suddenly.

"I thought you were with Jill," I said.

"Me? No. I just came along."

"She said you're her boyfriend."

Greg laughed. "That's news to me."

"I guess I really *don't* know much about you," I said.

I was outwardly calm, but thrilled inside.

"Why *don't* we leave?" I said at last.

Our courtship began then, and has never stopped in all the years since.

There were, however, challenges to overcome early in our relationship, among them the fact he was a Texan. I knew something about Texans: the Lone Star State was only fifteen miles south of my old hometown of Altus, just over the Red River. I knew from my youth that Texans suffer certain delusions, chief among them the feeling that they're better than everyone else, and that anything in Texas is better than anything anywhere else. We Oklahomans know better, of course.

My parents happened to be in Forth Worth when my mother, pregnant with me, began having labor pains; fortunately I was not born until after I was safely north of the border a week later. I evidently went to great lengths to be born in Oklahoma.

Despite the interstate rivalry, when it came down to it, I found that Greg shared with me the sense of values and community that I grew up with. Even my cooking was very similar to his mother's.

And yet we were in many ways opposites. While we shared an assertiveness and sense of humor, in other aspects we diverged. I admired in him his ruggedness and affinity for physical challenges, for his mechanical aptitude, his curiosity about how things worked, and his self-sufficiency, expressed especially in his ability to survive in the wilderness. He had serviced the rigors of military service, doing a tour in Vietnam as a medic. His outdoors sensibility was perfect for Southern California, with its year-round access to the wilds. He'd take me up in the mountains in his four wheel drive pickup truck, and we'd picnic and hike.

Meanwhile, Greg admired me for my free-spirited goofiness. Greg has always been a *cool guy*, always composed and image conscious, reluctant to display his vulnerable side. In contrast, I've never had a problem with being nerdy and making pig noises and goofy faces, of being laughed at. After a while, Greg began to take acting lessons, too, and as if to dramatize our differences, our acting teacher once gave us a unique assignment: come to the following class as our opposites: wardrobe, character, mannerisms. Greg came as a nerdy geek, and I as a tough street chick. It was a blast, and a revealing one at that.

Early on, Greg took me to see him work, and his job fit his personality perfectly. Hollywood may be largely make-believe, but stunt work, especially in the days before computer graphics, was anything but. It required physical strength, superb athleticism, quick thinking, quick reflexes and a sense of adventure.

The first time I saw him do stunt work, it was on the set of the television series *CHiPs*. He was doing car chases, taking turns being the chaser and the "chasee." I'd never realized what a big deal stunts could be, and how real they were when you weren't watching on the small (or big) screen. Soon enough, they became *too* real for me: I couldn't bear to watch him do a high speed roll off a pipe ramp, so I left the set.

In fact, after that day, I never actually saw Greg work again. Even the thought of what he was doing filled me with too much fear. I wound up waiting till the film or TV show came out in order to watch his work, with him sitting right beside me on the couch, and I could hug him and feel his presence and know he was safe.

About a month before my mother died—after I'd been seeing Greg for five months—I called her for guidance. She seemed the right person to ask, since she'd already given me good advice in choosing a mate: she had told my sister and me to marry a man who carries a pocket knife. *They're handy,* she'd say. *They know how to fix things.* Greg certainly qualified. But now I had a terrible problem: I was in love with him, but he never mentioned marriage.

"*I know just the thing*," she said.

I braced myself. "Yes, Mom?"

"Bake an apple pie!"

"A what?" I asked.

"An apple pie," she said. "I'll tell you how."

So I went to Greg's house to make him dinner while he was at work, and with the phone to my ear, my Mom told me, step by step, how to make the pie crust. As it baked, and its delicious scent filled the air, I realized with a smile the method behind my mother's apparent madness. It was a seduction, not sexual, but a loving one, the promise of a family, a safe place where the deepest kind of love could really blossom. The pie would serve as a guidepost to that, pointing Greg in the direction of a lifetime together with me.

While it baked, I prepared a full meal for him to complement it, and laid out the table with a tablecloth, and full place settings. As the time drew near my heart was racing. I carefully removed the pie from the oven to let it cool, and considered lighting candles but decided against it—I wanted to evoke family, not romance.

By the time he came through the door, I was a nervous wreck. He smiled when he saw what I'd done for him, and I wordlessly guided him to the table, where I pulled out his chair with a flourish.

And that's when it happened.

I lost my footing, reached out to the counter to keep from falling, and knocked the pie face down onto the linoleum.

I felt my insides collapse when I saw the wreckage of that pie. After a moment of shock I sank to my knees and started sobbing. Greg immediately got down and put his arms around me and held me close.

"Will you marry me?" he said suddenly.

I was sobbing too hard to say anything; I just nodded and we held each other.

Later that night, my mother called. "Did it work?" she asked. I couldn't tell a lie. *"Yes!"*

On August 16th, 1980, I was standing in the back yard of the beautiful Toluca Lake home of Karen Sund, wearing a wedding dress. Greg, standing tall in his tux, was next to me. and surrounding us were 350 of our closest friends. Beyond them, next to the aviary with exotic birds and peacocks and a pool set in an elaborate landscape, a band was ready to play on cue. Beyond all this was an expansive grassy lawn that rolled down in tiers toward the lake, with a table on each tier, so the deep, rich green of the grass was a vivid contrast to the white chairs and tablecloths.

Toluca Lake is a community just over the hill from Hollywood, and it was truly a "Hollywood wedding." Karen was heir to the "Don the Beachcomber" restaurant fortune, and we got to know her through a stunt coordinator named Bud Davis, who would hold court at a restaurant nearby called The Money Tree, a gathering place for stunt men and their wives. Greg would dine there at least once a week, and often several times, to relax after a strenuous day or network for the next job. Bud, who had given Greg so much work, was in fact one of the two Best Men at our wedding. For Bud, it was easy to get to the wedding—he lived in the guest house on Karen's property.

Other Hollywood denizens were there, mostly Greg's friends and coworkers, as he'd been in the business longer than I had, and was in fact ten years older than I.

There were also about twenty-five Texans—Greg's relatives, who came into town a few days before. Unfortunately, the timing of their early arrival was not ideal: since my mother had died eight months before our wedding day, it fell to Greg and me to do all the planning and attendant errands, purchases, phone calls and arrangements. We were practically in melt-down mode when his relatives showed up in need of attention, which stressed us out even more. The only thing that kept me going through the prenuptial frenzy was the thought of our planned honeymoon—in the Sequoias, where we'd be at peace.

The wedding itself was performed by the pastor of my church, Brian Crowe, with my father (who was Minister of Music at the church) singing. My father could have performed the ceremony himself, since he was ordained, but I felt it was better to honor my pastor by letting him preside, and allow my father simply to enjoy himself rather than be stressed out with the duties of the wedding ceremony.

I have come to regret the choice. My father enjoyed all of his weddings, and, though we never discussed it afterward, I think he would have loved to perform the ceremony for us.

Still, my father was up front in a tux, standing next to Brian during the proceedings, so in a way I had two ministers. And when the big moment arrived and we exchanged our vows, Pastor Crowe turned to the crowd and said, "And now, it gives me great pleasure—to let your *father* pronounce you husband and wife!"

So my father, quite surprised, took center stage and finished the job with a big smile on his face. That part was also a surprise to me—and it filled me with joy. The only thing missing was my mother; in that moment of exquisite happiness I thought of her. But Pastor Crowe, unknown to me, decided to include her in the ceremony. As soon as my father pronounced us husband and wife, Pastor Crowe read a passage from the Book of Hebrews that spoke of a "great cloud of witnesses," He explained that he felt that when our family members died, they were the witnesses in heaven, that they can see us from there.

In a bow to my mother's accent, Pastor Crowe said, "So right now, I believe there's a southern belle up there. And she is saying 'Well I *declare!*'"

The guests applauded, Greg and I kissed, and the celebration began. After dinner and much champagne, the guests danced around the pool, and despite the free flow of alcohol everywhere, no one fell in. The pool did not go to waste, though: my brother Jimmy, now nine years old, came equipped with a bathing suit and was the first one in, followed soon afterward by other children.

As we mingled with all the guests and thanked them, and danced the evening away, I began more and more to think about the decorated pickup truck with its luggage in place, ready to spirit us off to the mountains.

When that moment was near, Greg came to me with a troubled look on his face.

"Ready to go?" I said.

"Well, yes. Except…"

"Except what? What's wrong?"

"We are not going quite as far as we were kind of planning."

"How far are we going?"

"I got us a room at the Universal Sheraton, just up the road," he said, sheepishly.

"What is going on?" I demanded.

"Disneyland," he blurted out. "They want to see Disneyland."

"Who?"

"My folks. My family."

"So who's stopping them?"

"They want us to take them there."

I was incredulous. The day had been perfect! And suddenly this?

"Tell them we can't," I said.

"I already told them we would."

I was angry but kept a smile on my face as several more guests stopped by to say goodbye.

At nine o'clock we finally got into the pickup truck and trundled the two miles to the Sheraton, unloaded, and spent the night in a room on the same hallway as dozens of relatives, more than two hundred miles away from where I'd dreamed we would be.

The next day we went even further in the wrong direction: thirty-five miles south, back home to Anaheim, home of Disneyland. We did our best to entertain Greg's family, and while we got to hang out in the "wilds" of Adventureland, it was a far cry from the more pristine wilderness of the Sierra Nevada mountains. By late afternoon Greg and I finally made our escape.

It was a fitting place to spend the first—well, actually, *second* night of our marriage—among the Big Trees of Sequoia National Park. I was still relatively new to these things, but enthusiastic. The memory of my first visit to the Big Trees, a few years before, was still vivid. We had arrived not long after dawn. It was a bright, hot, dry time in California, but cool and damp and dark in the grove. Due to the nature of the leaves of the sequoia, the dew settles on them readily and drips down to the ground around them; they create their own rain showers. We hiked our way along paths and off of them, over and around huge logs and other vestiges of the wreckage of ancient trees. As we made our way along, Greg always pointed out a place where I might fall, waited to extend a hand, or even had me jump into his arms to get over a difficult spot.

At one point, my reach exceeded my grasp, or at least my leap exceeded my capacity to navigate it—from a particularly large log, on the edge of a steep hill. I decided to jump, then thought better of it, and balanced uncertainly. Greg quickly held out a hand to steady me, and when I slipped he caught me, and broke the fall. It's possible my story might have ended that morning if not for Greg's sureness and strength.

As events proved, Greg was always someone I could count on for such support, both physically and emotionally.

On the second night of our honeymoon, in a rustic amphitheater deep in the woods, a park ranger told us many things about the trees and the forest, but two facts stood out to me: one, they were over 2,700 years old, and two, they sprouted from the ashes of a great fire. I remembered thinking how beautiful and powerful that something so glorious could come out of ashes. My upbringing in faith had a way of framing my thoughts, and my reaction to this was no exception. The facts the ranger had shared with us worked in my brain and by morning, as we awakened in a tent to the fresh scent of pine and smoke from nearby campfires, I thought of Isaiah 61:3, which speaks of "beauty for ashes" and "trees of righteousness." I thought about when those words were supposed to have been written—over 2,700 years ago, the same time this great forest was being born from its own ashes. To this day, they are the oldest and largest living things on earth.

It would have been ideal to enjoy an extended stay in their midst, but we wound up combining business with pleasure during our honeymoon. Greg had landed the position of stunt coordinator for a Pia Zadora movie shooting in Vegas, so after several days in the wilderness we descended to that center of glitz and glitter in the pickup truck, rolled up our sleeves and got back to work.

The film shoot was very successful, and uneventful except for one incident that is illustrative of the kinds of people who inhabit the fringes of the entertainment world. The previous year, I had auditioned for the role of "Special Guest DJ" on a show starring Denny Terrio called *Dance Fever*. The audition was a real cattle call, with many gorgeous young women showing up. Into this intimidating situation, a young actress walked in, all glittered up.

"I've just flown in from Vegas," she announced without provocation. "I'm a special friend of Frank Sinatra's. You may as well all go home; I already have this job."

There was, needless to say, no general move toward the exit.

I hung in there, auditioned, and got the part. It was a Merv Griffin production, and working with Merv was a pleasure; he was a real gentleman, and very personable. There was another star on the show, short in stature, who proved something of a pervert. I was in a long skin tight black shiny body suit, like a disco outfit, and this guy kept coming up to me with his face in my crotch making propositions along the lines of "I could make you very happy."

Fortunately I was able to resist his "charms."

Flash forward a year later, and the girl who'd bragged so much at that audition showed up on the set in Las Vegas; she was the stand in for Pia Zadora. We all sat down on long tables on the set for lunch, and she was just really yakking it up about herself.

"It's so cool being Pia Zadora's stunt double," she bragged.

This was news to Greg, who was sitting across from her. Greg was the stunt coordinator—the person in charge of hiring stunt people —and he'd actually hired a woman named Janet Brady for that job.

I shot a look at Greg, but he just grinned.

"Is this your first time doing it?" he asked.

"Oh no," she said.

"And what do you do?" she asked.

"I'm the stunt coordinator," said Greg, slamming the trap shut.

She smiled, quite embarrassed, and, seeking to change the subject, quickly turned to me and said: "Don't I know you?"

"Yes," I said. "We met on the audition to *Dance Fever.*

60

"Right!" she said. "I wonder who ever got that job?"

"I did."

Upon our return from Vegas, Greg drove me to our own dream house, parked the truck, and prepared to carry me over the threshold. Now, I'd lived in simple houses in Oklahoma and California, and this was definitely moving up.

Not *up* in the sense of status or riches; rather, *up* in the sense of altitude—the house was in La Tuna Canyon, a hilly area just north of Los Angeles. The place itself was an old farmhouse—Greg affectionately referred to it as the Love Shack—which he rented for $150 a month prior to our wedding, after which point the farmer who owned it bumped up the rent to $250.

I suppose the farmer needed to boost the rent to compensate for the additional wear and tear my small feet would inflict on the place, though as I first laid eyes on it, it looked for all the world like it had plenty of wear and tear on it already, enough so that any more would likely bring it down. Greg said that if the termites ever stopped holding hands, the house would fall down.

It was red with white trim, built on a wooden foundation, with no insulation—basically wood siding on the outside and paneling on the inside. And it was sinking on one side. When I first entered the kitchen I staggered and almost lost my footing, because the floor was so misaligned with the walls.

Greg opened the faucet, gathered some water into his hand and poured it out onto the kitchen floor. It ran down to the lower end of the floor.

"See the advantage?" he explained. "If you spill something, it runs like a river to one side, so you always knew where to put the mop."

It was crude, but it did have its own "air conditioning" system: in the dining room, the wood paneling on the wall didn't meet up with the linoleum floor, so there was about one inch of daylight coming through that crack. A breeze could keep your feet cooler on a hot day.

The dining room even had green carpeting—after a fashion. Grass grew under the house, and long blades would pop up every day. Most people might sweep or vacuum before guests arrived, but I got into the habit of pulling up the grass and throwing it out as the last thing to do before answering the door.

It was harder to conceal the defect in the bathroom: a big hole in the floor around the toilet. It was convenient, if you wanted to view the ground beneath the house while on the throne, but otherwise it was rather annoying, especially when you sat down. Basically, the only thing holding the toilet in the house was the plumbing beneath it, so it had a tendency to teeter when used, giving the lucky user the sensation of falling through the floor while in the middle of a very intimate activity. The hole did have its advantages—if a male user had bad aim, or the toilet suffered an overflow, it didn't matter so much because the grass beneath the house could always use a little extra fertilizing.

Humble, yes. Laughably so.

But the fact is that I have nothing but fond memories of the place. I retained all my skill at sewing, and spent much time in the early days of our marriage sewing lace curtains, couch slip covers, and other things for the house. I decorated everything in floral, and wallpapered the kitchen (with some difficulty, as there seemed to be no right angles at all in the room). Greg loved the work I did; he had been a bachelor for a long time, and was very impressed with my feminine touch.

We didn't need much in those days to make us happy. Our house was a paradise to us, and our time there a time of bliss. But it wasn't the last chapter in the pages of our lives by any means; it was an early one, and though lofty in altitude among the Verdugo hills, it proved to be a place from which we leaped far higher than either of us had ever known or expected to know.

6. Taking Off

In August 1981, on our first anniversary, Greg drove me from our humble Love Shack to the Van Nuys Airport, a small facility in the middle of the San Fernando Valley, where an Arrow was waiting for me.

It was a *Piper* Arrow—a single engine low-wing airplane, gleaming white with a scarlet stripe down its length. He wanted to mark our anniversary by going to the site of our honeymoon—Sequoia National Park—this time in about an hours' travel time, rather than five hours in the car.

It had been an eventful year for him. He was, in a word, *prospering.* Greg was very good at his job, and stunt men were in demand, and that demand was huge. This was the age of *Smokey and the Bandit* and *Cannonball Run,* and numerous action television programs. It was a good time to make a living flipping through the air, crashing cars and falling out of buildings.

He decided to use some of his newfound riches to purchase an airplane and surprise me with it. He'd long ago learned to fly, as part of his military training, Soon we were airborne, winging out way north. As we reached the edges of Sequoia National Park, in the heart of the Sierra Nevada Mountains, I was suddenly struck by how lush and green they appeared. It's worth noting that most of California is brown—golden brown—one of the reasons for its moniker "The Golden State." It is an arid place for the most part, especially in August. But as the Sequoia National Forest spread out beneath us in a splash of undulating green, clinging to the edges of great mountains, I noticed the greenness, and thought of the phrase "salad days"—days of growth, of lushness, of life, innocence and perhaps even foolishness—truly this was the start of our salad days.

We landed safely, found our way to a picnic spot, commemorated our anniversary with a meal Greg had packed, then flew back home in time for the evening news.

It was the first of many such trips we took. Other couples might hop in a car in Los Angeles and travel up the Coast Highway for an hour or so to picnic in Ventura by the sea or Ojai nestled in the coastal mountains. Greg and I would hop into our plane for an hour or so and picnic instead in distant Yosemite or even Las Vegas, then return home by mid-afternoon, before earthbound mortals even got a chance to get stuck in rush hour traffic.

Our lives were literally soaring.

When it was time to visit Greg's family in Texas, we didn't have to do the two-day drive or take an airliner; we just traveled a couple of miles to Van Nuys Airport, hopped on the Arrow and flew. During these flights, I got to skim swiftly over the vast expanses of desert I used to gaze upon when I was a child on the bus, though of course the perspective was very different, in so many ways.

There were bumps along the way, of course; the desert could be a turbulent place, with updrafts and other sudden winds. Sometimes we were physically exhausted by the time we got to Austin, where Greg's family lived.

They were salad days indeed; we were green, and it was a time of learning dangerous lessons, too, as we spread our wings. On one occasion we were over Arizona after a tough flight with an unexpected headwind that had delayed us an hour. The sun had already set, and the desert was gaping blackly at us below. It was hard enough to make an emergency landing on a street or open field, but to try to set down after nightfall was basically suicide. Especially if you do it "dead stick"— i.e., without an engine. We were low on fuel.

According to our charts, there was supposed to be an airfield in the community of Avra Valley, outside Tucson, but we could see nothing below.

"Six Echo Charly on final for Avra Valley," said Greg into the radio microphone, announcing our call letters.

Only static greeted us.

"Avra Valley, this is Six Echo Charlie. Anybody there?"

Again silence, and our fears mounted.

"Avra Valley, please come in."

We were already on reserve fuel, and Greg started looking for alternative landing sites while he continued forlornly to call in over the radio. At last we spotted headlights crawling along the ground and discerned a highway. Greg began a descent to land on it, hoping there were no telephone poles or power lines to snag us.

At that point, a voice crackled over the radio: "Six Echo Charlie, Avra Valley here."

"Six Echo Charlie here, Avra!" said Greg.

"It's your lucky night. You just caught me. I was sweeping up and about to leave."

"Ten Four Avra. Can you flip on the lights?"

"Will do."

66

At once, the inky landscape below lit up with hundreds of lights, like Christmastime. The airfield was now readily visible, and Greg put us down smoothly within a few minutes, and at last we could relax.

After a year being airborne in the Arrow, we realized that while the plane was a great way to make distant places near, it posed for us a problem: what about quick access to places that didn't have a runway nearby? On our flights, we'd often pass over forest clearings and mountainside parks that we were tempted to explore, but were unable to access except by the old fashioned means: by car, and then on foot.

I realize this might sound a bit self-indulgent, but truth be told we were both self-indulgent during that time. So on our *second* anniversary, Greg provided us with a solution to our problem by augmenting our aircraft inventory with the addition of a Robinson R-22 helicopter.

Greg had initially trained as a helicopter pilot in the Army, but was denied serving in that role due to colorblindness. Now he applied his skills in a very different context. It was a simple two-seater, and was a joy to fly. Greg even let me take over the control stick at times, and he noted my gentle touch. It is said that women make better helicopter pilots than men, because controlling a chopper requires the application of constant, gentle, measured adjustments, and women seem more adept at such tasks than men, with their heavier hands and the inclination for greater abruptness.

Now it was possible to pack a picnic lunch (there was room for little else in the small craft) and take short hops to nearby sites. Once we had flown the Arrow over the Angeles National Forest and spotted a patch of lovely green on a mountaintop overlooking the small town of Fillmore. We thought back then what a great place that would be for a picnic—doubtless very pristine because of its inaccessibility to anyone but the hardiest of hikers.

We remembered that place after we got the R-22 and on a beautiful Saturday afternoon we flew there, made our landing, and cut the engine. We enjoyed the awesome silence of the primal wilderness, accessible so easily to us by helicopter, and with such difficulty to anyone else—mere mortals who would be forced to struggle up the slopes on foot.

Now it was picnic time, and though it may seem strange, I was still a thrifty shopper and avid couponer even as we spent $350 an hour to fly the helicopter. I'd spent so many years growing up being frugal that it was in my blood. I remember telling Greg what a deal I was able to get on the picnic lunch we brought—a $3.59 box of crackers for just fifty cents. He smiled and probably thought I was crazy, but I'd had to live a thrifty life for so long that setting aside those concerns was not easy for me.

Greg carried our picnic basket to a rock not far from the helicopter, and the two of us ate and cuddled in the idyllic setting—alone in the pristine wilderness, and much in love. It was all perfect till we heard laughter, then a groan, then the sound of someone hushing someone else up.

We immediately sprang to our feet, me ready in my Kung Fu stance, and Greg holding a stick with which to bop anyone who came near. Before we knew what was happening, we discovered the place was alive with young people, partying hearty with beer, pot and munchies. They'd all hidden when they heard our helicopter, assuming it was some sort of police raid.

Upon closer examination, the place was full of trash—evidently it was a popular partying spot, not nearly as inaccessible as we'd thought. After initial annoyance, we hung out with the kids and shared some of our picnic lunch.

With two aircraft counted among the family's assets, we decided that it was time to say 'goodbye' to the Love Shack. Three days after our second anniversary, we closed escrow on our first house, in the San Fernando Valley community of Panorama City. We owned two cars, two aircraft, and now a house. We were prospering.

But we did pay a price for that prosperity. Most of our wealth was coming from Greg's work, and I have to say, his very occupation gave me the same sorts of fears that my mother's illness had given me growing up. Whatever exuberance we may have felt from each other, from our youthful enthusiasm for life and our expensive toys, was tempered by a sense of lurking danger. When Greg was with me, I'd squeeze him tightly, to remind me that he was alive, well, and safe.

We made a tacit agreement to keep his work as far from my mind as possible. On a typical day, we'd be enjoying each others' company at home, and then suddenly he'd get up and get ready to go. I'd avert my eyes and otherwise distract myself while he prepared for whatever stunt he was planning to do, packing his Nomax suit and fire gel, for instance, in case of a fire burn, or getting into pads for what was likely a motorcycle stunt, or loading his "5-point" racing belt for a car jump. It was "magical thinking," I know—the childlike belief that if I didn't see it, it wasn't happening.

And it didn't work—I would still worry. But ignoring the reality of what he was about to do helped me cope with the anxieties. I tried not to think about it, and that was something Greg encouraged me to do, and he told me white lies to alleviate my fears.

"So what are you doing today?" I might casually ask, as a wife might about her husband doing real estate deals or fixing autos.

"Oh, just some chases," he might reply, knowing that would make me think he would just be driving a car running from the cops, which is dangerous, but not as dangerous as other endeavors. We had a system of denial, and for what it was, it got us through.

Though inevitably there were glitches.

One day, a stunt coordinator called, and Greg wasn't home.

"Tell Greg I want him to come an hour early tomorrow," he said, "so we can check out the rig he'll be using to do the thing between the two buildings."

A perfect way to ruin a nice afternoon. I did my best to suppress my fears on the matter, but when Greg came home, I asked him, "*What* thing between the two buildings?"

"Oh," he said, caught off-guard. "I'm just going across on a cable."

"How tall are these buildings?" I demanded.

"Oh, just two stories or some such," he said.

It turns out they were 14-story twin towers in Long Beach. He went across hanging with his hands. *Twice.* Once by himself for the cameras below, and again with a helmet camera for the point of view shot the director wanted.

This was not the most dangerous stunt he did by any means, but it tormented me the rest of the day, till he got home at night and I could see with my eyes that the worst fears of my imagination had not come true.

My emotional contact with Greg's career was mostly one of fear, but I was proud as well, because what he did was difficult, and he did it so well. One favorite of mine was his "Reverse Rollover," because no one had ever done it before, and we don't think it's ever been done since. It takes a lot of skill to roll a car using a pipe ramp, going forward, but to be able to hit it just right, and at the right speed and angle, *in reverse*, is not for amateurs, nor even for most professionals.

Greg also did beautiful "4 wheel drifts," 360's and 180's, just like a dance.

My favorite stunt of his, in terms of finesse and the element of danger, was his "motorcycle T-Bone." I have a picture of that one on the wall in our house. A "T-Bone" is a stunt involving one car striking another broadsided—perpendicular to one another—hence the "T." It's a rough hit, because it's such a quick stop for the car doing the hitting. But at least the driver of a car has safety belts to keep him in place, a crash helmet, and the engine and body of the car to absorb the shock and cushion the blow.

Not so if done on a motorcycle, and that's what Greg did. He didn't even wear a crash helmet because the plot of the CHiPs episode involved a guy who joyrided with no helmet, so it was central to the stunt that he *not* wear one.

Of course, they did not simply expect him to plow bodily into a car, with no helmet—that would have been dangerous.

Instead, the plan was for him to hit a car, flip through the air up and over it and land about thirty feet on the other side, on pavement. Without a helmet.

Obviously if I'd known what the plan was, I would have done all I could to stop the madness, but per our *m.o.*, he told me nothing about it till after the fact.

It was an incredible stunt, and many younger stunt men were there to watch the pro, and ask questions about his preparation. He padded only on his left side, and a little under his wig, which wouldn't have done much if he hit his head. But he knew he would keep his head off the ground; he was like an acrobat in that respect.

The young guys were shocked that he only padded his left side; they asked why not the right too? He said that he was going to land on his left side, holding his head up, and explained that if you don't know exactly how you will land, and on what side of your body, you had no business doing the stunt.

It went off exactly as planned, though he ultimately paid a high price. He had a huge, oozing, bloody "strawberry" on his left hip for weeks afterward, and has suffered pain in his hips ever since. He still has about a three inch scar.

7. My "Glamour" Years

While Greg was busy battering and bruising his body to contribute to our growing prosperity, I took a very different route in making my own contribution. By 1981 I was a rising young starlet, landing commercials and guest starring roles on television and in feature films.

One of my most memorable early experiences was a guest star appearance I landed on an ABC TV series called *Open All Night,* starring George Dzundza and Bubba Smith. We rehearsed all week, the last few days on the stage. When I made my entrance and delivered my first line with the audience that Friday night, it was electrifying. I didn't know the line was so funny until we got the audience's reaction; they were roaring through the whole scene.

I was overwhelmed; it felt like a coming together of all my theatricality, all my stage experiences, my performances before audiences and before my family, from my earliest memories, to that point. I would have had a recurring role had the series gotten picked up; unfortunately, it only last thirteen episodes. But I was now more determined than ever to find a life in the performing arts.

There remained, of course, reconciling the iniquities of Hollywood with my upbringing of faith, but once I accepted show business as my career, it was just a matter of making sure Hollywood conformed to my moral sensibilities, and not the other way around. I did this chiefly by being upfront with the people I worked with. I let my manager know that I wouldn't utter vulgar language, and that nudity was out of the question. Anyone who hired me knew these were the conditions under which I worked.

After my exhilarating experience on *Open All Night,* I told my agent I loved multi-camera TV with a live audience, and soon thereafter I landed a guest star appearance on *Happy Days.* I introduced Greg to Henry Winkler— "the Fonz." Greg was overwhelmed—he said Henry was the biggest star he had ever met.

In 1981, I landed a role on a pilot for a CBS sitcom called *Kudzu,* directed by Rod Daniels. It was a co-starring role in the series, and I played the role of a beauty contest wannabe: each week I was to be practicing for a talent presentation for some local beauty contest. It was not atypical of the kinds of roles I was being cast in at that time, and the scene I played was illustrative.

In the pilot, I was preparing for the Miss Mozell County contest, and I was learning the fire baton, so I kept going into the local store to buy kerosene, in my red sparkly baton twirler outfit. While I was practicing twirling, Kudzu, the guy who was in love with me (played by Tony Decker), began to make a confession to me about being illegitimate. His phrasing was something like, "Veranda, would it matter to you if I told you that I don't know who my Daddy is?"

Just looking at myself twirling in the mirror, I answered, "I could care less."

He said to the others in the general store, "She's standing by her man!" which was to be his ongoing fantasy in the sitcom, though I would never actually pay him any mind.

Then he said, "Veranda, I really want to thank you for your loyalty."

At that, I spun around, and, using my baton to simulate a microphone, said "Loyalty! It is my fervent desire to visit every city and hamlet in this wonderful country. And to say to my fellow citizens therein... Loyalty is not *tacky!* Thank you!"

With that I turned and walk out with my baton and kerosene. Then there is a shot of the three of them standing there dumbfounded.

It was in truth a stretch for me—the straight-*A* student, graduated from the Mentally Gifted Minors program, playing an airhead. But I had the look, and it was fun, so I did what I could to be convincing. In this I was aided by an acquaintance—a model and girlfriend of a stunt man, who was quite stuck on herself and her beauty, and who provided an ideal role model for me. She was the type who would come to a party, looking absolutely stunning, and sidle up to me and gush forth with compliments: "Teri, you are looking *so* beautiful today!"—just fishing for flattery in return. I rarely cooperated in that respect, but knowing her paid dividends: I used her as a role model for many of the characters I played.

Unfortunately, the executives at CBS were not as fond of *Kudzu* as we were, and the series was never picked up.

But my character lived on, in many incarnations and bit parts. One was in the 1982 film *Pandemonium,* a comedy that also featured Judge Reinhold, Phil Hartman and Tom Smothers. I played, in essence, the same character as in *Kudzu*—a self-absorbed dumb blonde practicing my beauty contest speeches.

The film itself was not long, but the film shoot was, and it featured a large cast, and I got to know many of my fellow actors. Among these was Paul Rubens, who was just then working out his Pee-Wee Herman character (which he did not play in the movie).

I did get to meet Pee-Wee, though: Greg and I went to see "The Pee-Wee Herman Show" at the Roxy one night during a break in the filming. We had no idea what that was, and had never heard of Pee-Wee Herman. Paul Rubens came out on stage in the opening of the show, tossing Tootsie rolls.

"Anybody want some candy?" he giggled.

Then, gradually, he started throwing them to people a little harder, until he was throwing them *at* people. Then we were all under the tables and ducking, as he was beaning us and hitting the walls, screaming *"Ricochet!"*

It was obviously the start of something big.

Certainly Paul thought so; he told me he was planning to do a movie featuring this odd, fussy man-boy character, and that he wanted me to be in it. I was flattered by this compliment, and assured him I'd love to appear with him.

For the most part, my experience in the shooting of *Pandemonium* was one of joyful chaos, but it also tested me and the limits of my comfort with the raunchier aspects of Hollywood. Many times during the shoot, I would receive last-minute script rewrites, which would arrive at my door late the night before the scene was scheduled. These inevitably contained objectionable material, and lead to sleepless nights for me, and an early morning call to my manager, who would then have to let the director know I wouldn't do the offensive material. At this point, they'd either go back to original script, do some other scene or postpone shooting.

While I was for the most part successful in parrying their attempts to violate my sense of propriety, in one devious incident, they got their way. In that particular scene, a college boy was supposed to put his hand over my name tag and then try to guess my name. The director wanted to make a gag out of it, by placing the name tag (and thus his hand) directly on my breast, something *not* in the script. I refused, and insisted on placing the nametag higher, near my collarbone. At last, they agreed.

During the filming, though, the actor put his hand too low. I was uncomfortable with where his hand was, but I carried on and we played the scripted guessing game, with him listing off various names, and me giggling and saying 'no' to each one.

He finally guessed "Mandy."

I said, "Right."

At this, he abruptly grabbed my breast and said, "Let me guess what school you're from." That was not in the script and not rehearsed. But unfortunately, I was so shocked, and as a young actress, always taught to play out a scene, I giggled and ran off. I realized immediately I'd been played for a fool, and if I'd been a more seasoned actress, I would have quickly stepped out of character to intentionally "flub" the scene, rendering it useless. But I stayed in character, and they got a look of genuine surprise from both actress and character, and it wound up in the movie. The actor and the director both laughed hysterically for what they'd accomplished, and I felt very bitter.

But that was not the worst of it.

Later that day, this actor came to me with tears in his eyes and told me how sorry he was that he'd conspired to disregard my wishes and cheat me of my dignity. I put my arms around him and told him it was okay.

That was about twenty minutes before I heard him laugh again, this time in an adjacent room, telling some of the cast that he just gave the greatest performance of his career, pretending to be sorry to me for what he'd done.

I stormed into the room and told him off, and have never spoken to him again. I feel, though, that the look of surprise on his face as I told him off was even more believable than his sob-story performance he'd done for me.

To my surprise, despite the tensions on the set of *Pandemonium,* the director sought me out for a role in a television comedy pilot featuring Phil Hartman called *Cheeseball,* in which I landed the part of a Goldie Hawn-type sketch girl. In this, I wore a skimpy outfit but nothing too revealing. I suppose that even though they thought me a prude, I was funny enough to call upon again.

My minor appearance in *Pandemonium* seemed to fit in to an ascending pattern of movie and television appearances, leading to an audition for a part in a movie starring Dustin Hoffman. I was up for the role of Sandy, an aspiring actress in New York City, and Dustin Hoffman's girlfriend.

I breezed through the preliminary audition and was invited to read with Dustin, who greeted me at the studio offices, wearing jeans and a regular crew neck T-shirt. We had a great read together, and for some reason—could it have been my family's tradition of tricks and games? Or tradition of food fights?—I picked up some grapes from a bowl on the table and started throwing then at him during the reading. He started throwing some back; we got on very well, and he told me I was great for the part and he hoped to work with me.

I went home that night with my head full of thoughts of what I would wear to the opening of the film, the new friends and experiences I'd make when I vaulted to the top echelon of Hollywood talent, how I would thank my father and mother at the Oscars.

My hopes for the film were not far off—it did go on to win an Oscar and garnered several nominations—but the hopes for myself were a bit over-optimistic. Dustin himself called me personally that night and told me they'd decided to go with a name actress for the role of Sandy: Teri Garr.

The film was *Tootsie*.

By early 1984, something began to stir inside me—something new, something exciting, something I'd never felt before, and something that, without my realizing it, signaled the sunset of my aspirations for a glamorous career.

That something was my son Joe.

I did not have any expectations that things would change as a result of my pregnancy, and in fact shortly before I was due I got a call from Paul Rubens about auditioning for the part of Dottie, his girlfriend, in a movie called *Pee-Wee's Big Adventure*.

It was a challenging audition, to say the least: I was in early labor when I read for the part, waiting between five- to seven-minute contractions to perform. Ultimately, they thought it too risky to have me in a big role just weeks after my first child was be born. They wound up casting Elizabeth Daily in the role.

Joe was born, after a rough labor and c-section, on December 28, 1984—five years to the day of my mother's death, and eleven years from the day our house burned to the ground.

I had expected that things would return somewhat to normal after he was born. Naturally I was aware that such a gift from God is a life-changing event. But I had been on stage or screen in one form or another since I was five, and had no expectation I would be anywhere else in the future.

Still, after failing to land the part of Dottie, it began to dawn on me that change was afoot. I was still young, but not the bubbly young teenage type I had so adroitly mastered over the years. I was also a mother; I'd put on a bit of weight, but it was more a maturation than anything physical. I had gone through a subtle transformation.

I had been pursuing my professional acting career for four years, with increasing levels of success; in fact, I was living a charmed life, because although I wanted to succeed, I never hungered for it the way so many of my fellow actors did. My acting career, and the successes I enjoyed, came to me. Sure, I wanted it, but I never worked too hard. In 1985, after years of easy success, and with a baby boy in my arms, I stopped trying altogether, and success stopped coming.

Appropriately enough, I did land one acting role that year—a one-day appearance on *Days of Our Lives*. For once I was not a bubbly cheerleader or a beauty pageant contestant. I played Patch's *mother.*

Being a mother was indeed my new role, and that appearance on *Days of Our Lives* was the last one I ever played on film or television.

Greg kept working, though, as actively as ever. In fact, thanks to Greg, little Joe was a very well-traveled baby during the first year of his life. He flew with us twenty-two times that year, all over the country, for location film shoots. Greg was making steady money, and I was busy mothering.

The year culminated with a two month stay at the Radisson Hotel in Tel Aviv, Israel, while Greg did stunt work in Jaffa for the Chuck Norris film *Delta Force*. While terrorism was a reality in Israel at that time, it was not as prominent in the lives of Israelis as it is now. But 1985 saw an escalation in the number of bombing attacks, and after we'd been there a few weeks, we heard bombs exploding in the vicinity of our hotel. Very quickly, Americans in Tel Aviv became very keen on getting out, but the airports were jammed and flights out were impossible to get.

The next few weeks I spent there, people became increasingly paranoid. Unattended baggage was instantly viewed with distrust. It seemed the reality of everyday activity became wildly distorted, and any unexplained, unattended inanimate object became a potential cause of mayhem and death.

Because I was a young mother with an infant son, I was given relatively high priority for a ticket back home, and decided to leave as soon as I could, even though Greg had to stay behind to finish the film. It was wrenching to leave him behind, and I could only hope that the strong survival skills he'd exhibited for so many years in his dangerous profession would see him through this new and very daunting threat.

The airport was a madhouse, with lines of people and luggage snaking around barriers, and heavily-armed Israeli Defense Force soldiers keeping a watchful eye over everything. Despite the high level of security—or perhaps *because of it*—everyone was jittery. As I neared the ticket counter, holding Joe tightly in my arms, I noticed a camel standing close by.

A stuffed camel.

It had long lashes, a goofy grin, and soft fur, and was life sized —taller than I was. Normally I wouldn't be alarmed by a stuffed camel, however large he might be, but this one had one problem: it was unattended.

Was it filled with explosives?

A terrorist Trojan Horse?

I shouted with my loudest stage voice: "Hey, whose camel is this?"

Instantly people spread out from the camel in the middle of the room and crouched against the far walls.

After a few moments of nervous silence, footsteps could be heard and a harried looking man in a business suit appeared, uttering what sounded like apologies in some Middle Eastern tongue. He picked up the camel and carried it quickly away.

Shortly thereafter, I made it safely on the plane with Joe, and no further stuffed camel problems arose.

It was a relief to get back onto U.S. soil, but also disappointing, because with the exception of a few weekends doing charity work in Mexico when I was younger, my experience of Israel had been my first outside the United States. Just as I was getting used to the rhythms and customs of a foreign land, my experience had been cut short, under such unfortunate circumstances.

Greg returned a month later—the longest month of my life— and at last our family was whole again.

In the twilight of my "glamour years" I played the role of a young mother, quietly raising my son, while Greg continued to work, and our path was laid out before us, and it was a good path. In 1988 we decided to sell our house in Panorama City and buy our dream property in the Santa Monica Mountains near Calabasas, a community on the western edge of the San Fernando Valley, where we would build in beautiful, rustic surroundings.

We had to wait for the necessary clearances from the California Coastal Commission in order to start construction, because the land was in a Coastal Zone, where development is highly regulated. In the meantime, we rented a small house in Reseda, halfway between Panorama City and Calabasas, in the heart of the Valley.

It seemed we were just a few scant months from paradise.

8. The Reseda Years

I have come to realize over the years that it is fairly easy for something to go wrong and yet go unnoticed till a minor problem becomes life-threatening.

It can happen in a very simple and straight-forward way; for example, in a flight Greg and I took in our Arrow from Los Angeles to the mountain community of Columbia, California early in our marriage. About halfway there, Greg started to notice something different about how the plane was handling. He couldn't put his finger on it; the instruments were fine, so we assumed everything was in order. We flew on as evening came on, two human beings in a fragile craft two miles above a darkening earth, held aloft by the forces of wind and the hand of God.

Just before nightfall, Greg decided to land at an airfield in Madera, a small community eighty miles short of our destination and check out the plane just to be sure. We pulled up to the hangar and before we'd even cut off the power, the look on the mechanic's face told us something was very wrong.

When we climbed out, we discovered that the entire right side of the plane was covered with motor oil. The engine had been within a few minutes of failure, and arriving at a strange airport at dusk with no power would have been a risky proposition.

We caught the error before disaster struck, and though we were laid up for a while during the repair process, we eventually got back home and continued on the course we were headed in our lives.

But in the late 1980s we went off course in a more subtle and profound way. Just as the birth of Joe signaled the end of my acting career, so the purchase of our dream home signaled the end of that dream and so many others. We wound up beset by unexpected economic turbulence: Greg stopped getting work. And worse—we didn't know it till too late. The problem was that even in the best of times, work can be sporadic in his field, so it's hard to judge if a bout of unemployment is just that—a bout—or if it is the end of a career.

We did have an inkling of trouble ahead, and the tangled tale that unfolded in 1988 laid bare so much that could go wrong in professional relationships, friendships and marriage.

In the stunt business, as in much of the entertainment world, you are hired by your friends. You have to network. And if you hire someone that another stunt coordinator doesn't like, you may never work for that stunt coordinator again. It's extremely political.

One of the stunt coordinators who gave Greg a lot of work had a rather unusual relationship with a woman who was also a friend of ours. They were married, but they lived in different houses, and were "separated," but they were always at The Money Tree together. They made out. They bought a house in Oxnard near the beach together. They looked like a married couple in all the years that we knew them.

In 1988 they went through a nasty divorce, and in the process, the stunt coordinator made the claim that he had not been with her for twenty years. I didn't know the particulars, but it appeared that the

84

stunt coordinator was not being wholly truthful about his relationship with this woman in an attempt to limit her claims on his estate. And worse, because he had so much power as a stunt coordinator, his wife became a pariah. Mutual friends stopped hanging out with her or even speaking to her out of fear of reprisal. And she was unable to get anyone to testify on her behalf, even though all she wanted anyone to do was simply assert the truth: that the two had been together on occasion during the last twenty years.

It was in this context that she came to our house one evening, very distraught. We showed her in and tried to comfort her.

"I understand why people will not testify," she said. "He is powerful and they'll suffer loss. And that's why I understand why you would not want to, even though I see you as truth tellers."

Her feelings about us cut us to the bone. How could we live with ourselves if we did not step forward now and help out our friend, who needed someone who was willing to speak the truth?

As we showed her out, the gathering gloom of evening reinforced our impression of her desperation.

"What do you want to do?" Greg asked as he closed the door.

"I want to testify," I said.

"It would mean the end of my career," he said.

"We can't be completely sure. Things may turn out all right for us."

"I *can* be pretty sure," he said. "But I don't want to run in fear. Fear from the truth."

"Neither do I," I said. We sat together for a while. At last, I added: "Can we live with ourselves if we don't?"

"No."

The next day I called her, and a few days later we went to her attorney's office and answered very simple, straightforward questions, along the lines of whether or not we'd seen them together during the past twenty years, and if so, how often.

I answered truthfully against the stunt coordinator, who wound up losing some of his property to her. We hurt him, and surely as night follows day, he turned around and hurt us. He stopped hiring Greg, and went around telling everyone that we lied. He also made it clear to others that if they hired Greg, he'd place them on his blacklist as well.

Worked dropped off almost immediately, but we battled back; Greg had other resources, producers who did not work with that stunt coordinator. Greg ran shows himself as a stunt coordinator, and was coordinating a number of stunts for Alan Landsburg, who was doing many Movies of the Week at that time. Unfortunately, "runaway production" to Canada became a problem in the late '80s, as producers sought to make their movies cheaper where the dollar was strong. When Landsburg packed up and moved his operation to Canada, we suffered considerable hardship.

Still, Greg continued to get some work. The drop-off was gradual, and through it all we were able to believe that it was a temporary lull, that the prosperous days would be back soon enough.

Not soon enough, though, for us to keep the helicopter. We took our last flight to Ojai in late 1988 before turning over the keys to an opportunistic buyer with cash. By then it needed plenty of maintenance; we received little for it, and the financial gain we had was mostly due to saving on storage space.

In 1989 we took our last flight on the Arrow 200 to Texas, to visit Greg's family. On the return trip across the Mojave, the golden sun was setting before us. Down below I saw it casting the longest, deepest shadows of any I could recall on any flight. The day was ending and heralding, in its ending, the end of much of what we'd known.

When we landed back at Van Nuys airfield, we literally taxied it up to the buyer, who was waiting anxiously. Appropriate to the then-current motif of endings, a few weeks later we found out that the fellow wrecked the plane on a bad takeoff. He was unhurt, but the plane was totaled.

During these increasingly difficult times, even when we got a break, things could go terribly wrong. The biggest fear for a stuntman's wife is to have the Stunt Coordinator come to your house at the end of the day, instead of your husband. This is precisely what happened when Greg was doing some stunt work for a TV series. It is a night I shall never forget, and that Greg will never remember.

It knocked his memory right out of him.

He was on the set, driving fast in a car while jumping over some other cars. Somehow his head hit the roll bar, even though he was in a five-point seat belt and had a helmet on.

It really rang his bell.

He didn't move immediately after the stunt was over, so the stunt coordinator, a guy named Paul, shook him, very concerned.

At last Greg stirred. "So when are we doing the stunt?" he asked earnestly, and a little confused.

Paul immediately turned to an assistant. "Get him in the ambulance!"

I had no idea that Greg had been hurt; I just figured he was working overtime, which he did often. Late that night Paul came to my door, and it struck fear into my heart. Behind him, I saw Greg staggering to get out of the car. Paul rushed over to help him, and I followed.

Greg definitely didn't look himself.

"What's wrong?" I asked Greg.

He looked at me blankly, without recognition.

"Greg?" I asked, terror coming over me.

"He'll be all right," Paul reassured me, but he didn't sound reassured himself.

"My little wife-y," Greg suddenly grinned to me vacantly.

"See?" said Paul. "He recognizes you."

"Where are we?" said Greg, looking around at the home we'd been living in for several months.

"What happened?" I demanded of Paul, seeing that asking Greg would be of little use.

Paul handed me a stack of papers marked St. Joseph Hospital – Emergency Room, told me about the incident on the set and the trip to the hospital. Greg had refused to stay there, even though the doctors urged him to. They were right. He didn't even know my name.

The documents instructed me to wake him at intervals throughout the night, and ask him simple factual questions—such as his Social Security number, address, phone number—and this I did, during a long and very traumatic vigil.

He wasn't able to answer *any* of my questions.

The documents instructed me to call the hospital if he couldn't answer them. When I did, they were angry with me for allowing Greg to leave the hospital at all, as if I had anything to do with the decision.

It was horrible.

The next day, I took him to see a neurologist, who examined Greg in my presence, then turned to me and spoke bluntly while Greg sat in the chair, looking mentally challenged. The doctor told me that Greg had suffered a severe trauma to his brain, and that I had to be prepared to take care of him in this state for the rest of my life.

Our world came crashing down.

I suddenly saw before me a different life from the one we'd set out to live just a few years before.

The doctor told me that if I was lucky, Greg might regain some of his brain function, and that it was possible he'd fully recover. It was simply difficult to know.

Weighed down with these fears, tempered slightly by the doctor's late reassurances, I made several more appointments and proceeded to work with Greg during the next few weeks. By the end of the month, he had improved considerably, and in six months' time his recovery was complete.

But naturally, our finances continued to deteriorate.

Through these increasingly lean times, we continued to pay not only rent at our home in Reseda but the mortgage on our property in Calabasas. We'd intended to build our dream house there in 1989 and move in by 1990, but we were held up by continuing legal entanglements with the Coastal Commission.

I scrambled to help as best I could. I took on some wardrobe design and sewing jobs for a TV commercial costumer. I made a giant carrot costume for a child actor, a walking chandelier costume, and a wedding dress that would break away when grabbed and pulled. I even worked on the set of one show for a few days, running in with needle and thread to re-sew a button, or make similar repairs. I would also do standard costumer work like pressing clothes and tagging them.

This work proved too sporadic, so I started working part-time in the school district as soon as Joe was old enough to attend school. I landed a job as an assistant administrator of the music program for elementary schools within the Los Angeles Unified School District. Those of us who worked in this capacity were not employees of the school district—which would have garnered us better pay and benefits

—we were instead subcontractors, paid through grants, Parent Teacher Associations, or, in wealthy areas, by parents paying for enrollment. The job did dovetail with my musical background. We oversaw the music program in twenty-six schools, and I was partly in charge of hiring, training, and over-seeing personnel who taught music appreciation. I also did some teaching. Overall, the job helped a little, and the reconnection with music was gratifying, but it was not enough to relieve our financial stress.

Meanwhile, Greg was out networking for stunt work, going to meetings, putting in bids for stunts—and coming up with nothing for his efforts.

On an autumn day in 1988, I took my many gnawing worries with me to the Anaheim Vineyard, a huge church not far from where I used to live when I was in high school. Halfway through the service, I stopped being at the service.

Which may sound strange, but that's the way it happened.

As the pastor delivered his sermon, I looked out the window behind the altar, and saw that the sun had set abruptly.

During a morning church service the sun had set.

In the dim light I saw a canyon, several miles long, fading into fog in the distance. It wasn't a canyon carved out of solid rock, but seemed more like a cityscape—I was looking down a canyon of incredibly tall buildings, their millions of windows twinkling brightly, creating what seemed like a river of light pouring down from them and onto the streets below, a swirling torrent of light gushing in rapids and eddies around people—countless thousands of people walking the sidewalks.

These people seemed unperturbed by the chaos of light; they appeared to be preoccupied. I could not make out their faces; for, despite the brightness, they seemed deep in shadow, indistinct, darkened figures; faceless, mere silhouettes.

There was a desperation in the way they carried themselves that suggested to me they were hungry.

I was on a kind of platform in front of them, and their hands were held out to me. I was touched by their hunger. I cried, "Oh, God what can I do for them?"

At this, food came pouring out of my chest and into their hands —the hands of countless thousands of hungry people—amidst a crescendo of exploding light.

And then I was back in Anaheim, and it was morning, and the service was over, and my sister Karen was nudging me.

"Are you all right?" she asked. You've been staring out the window during the whole service. I figured you were praying. I didn't want to bother you."

I stood up, quite disoriented, and assured her I was fine. It wasn't until over an hour afterward that I was able to talk to her, or anyone else, about what I'd been through, and even then it was perplexing, both the experience and its content. I had fears of my family going hungry, but in the "vision" I was the one feeding hungry ones. Surely I had been involved all my life in charitable work, so perhaps this element of my life experience brought on the vision. But I'd lived my whole life in small towns and suburbs, and hoped to settle at last in the rustic landscape of the Santa Monica Mountains, and had never been—and didn't plan to be—an urban dweller. So what was the meaning of the cityscape?

The experience haunted me for weeks afterward, for I was given to trying to understand these kinds of experiences, plumbing them for meaning. I came away with the strong feeling that I needed to feed the hungry, somehow, some way. The next week at church a plea

91

was put out for volunteers for Tree of Life Ministries, an organization in the San Fernando Valley that delivered food to familes in need, many of them in crisis, with children going hungry. I was sure this would be the fulfillment of the vision. For the next eight years on Mondays, as precarious as our situation was becoming, I delivered food to the needy for Tree of Life. I saw many who were in far worse condition than ours: mothers with young children abandoned by their husbands and fathers; others who'd suffered a tragedy of illness, earthquake (the earthquake of 1994 struck in the heart of the Valley) or fire that deprived them of health or home, and the ability to regain either, or elderly men and women who had no one to turn to for support.

But the odd thing was, I saw all their faces, and I wondered why I could not see their faces in my vision. I could make no sense of that part of the puzzle.

My immediate family was suffering through some tough times, but the late 1980s were hard on my extended family as well. Two years after my mother died, my father married Nancy, a widow who brought her two sons, Steven and Peter, into the family. They experienced unexpected and severe conflict while attempting to "blend" their families. In typical fashion, my father not only stuck to the relationship and worked hard, under the guidance and inspiration of prayer, to make it work, he also used it as the basis of a new direction in his own ministry. He and Nancy began to counsel couples with a series called *How to Stay Married and Love It!* and later published a book by that title.

Though my sister and I had moved out by that time, my younger brother Jimmy remained at home and suffered through the difficult experience. He would occasionally take refuge from the strife

92

by staying with Greg and I in the early days of our marriage, and we enjoyed having him. In particular, he came often during the time that we lived at the Love Shack. Greg bought him a dirt bike and taught him how to ride it when he was about eight years old. We'd take hikes in the canyon, went on picnics, went camping, took helicopter rides, went inner-tubing in Tujunga, and lots of other fun activities.

On one occasion, when we lived in Panorama City, Jimmy wanted to go camping. We pitched our little three-man dome tent in the front yard. That night, the Santa Ana winds came through, and rocked us till dawn. When we emerged in the morning, a huge limb of a tree—about ten or twelve inches in diameter—had fallen off the tree and landed right beside our tent.

It really would have hurt us if it had landed just a foot closer.

Such was Jimmy's closest brush with disaster during those early years, but in 1990, he suffered a disaster much more profound: that fall, when he was nineteen, he was busted for possession of crystal methamphetamines and served jail time. His addiction was an unfortunate offshoot of losing our mother at a young age, and family turmoil. When Jimmy was released, he came to live with us for a while. Even though we were embroiled in our own troubles, Greg showed a lot of patience and love for him.

Once, Jimmy's Toyota truck had broken down. The engine needed rebuilding, but he didn't have any money. Greg told him he'd help him out, and Jimmy was excited at the prospect of getting the cash needed to get his truck up and running.

He was thus surprised when, instead of handing him money, Greg handed him a wrench and told him to lift the hood: Greg was going to help Jimmy in the way his dad had taught him.

Greg examined the engine and said, "Take off these bolts here, and put the parts in this box. And when you're done, let me know."

A half hour later, Jimmy came back into the house looking for Greg, the job completed. Greg then instructed him to do the same thing with other engine parts, until by late in the day, Jimmy had disassembled the engine and its parts were lined up in about eight boxes along the driveway.

Jimmy was nervous throughout the week that they worked on it —afraid he would never see his truck whole again, but Greg gave him no choice. The two went through all the parts. He showed Jimmy how to repair those that could be repaired, and they replaced whatever couldn't. Afterward, Greg had him put it all together again.

On the seventh day, Greg told Jimmy to get into the driver's seat and said, "Okay—turn it over."

I can still remember the big grin on Jimmy's face as the engine jumped to life; he was ecstatic. Jimmy had rebuilt that engine, something of which he would never have believed he was capable. And in the tradition of the Peach Seed Monkey, Greg had taken something of little value—a broken down truck—and delivered from it a gift, not just of a truck that was now fixed, but of the know-how to fix one.

Into the gathering gloom of our lives in early 1992 came a bright light: my second son Christian was born on March 31. Our family's conditions upon his arrival were so very different from those that greeted Joe, when we were at the height of worldly success. As joyful as his birth was, Christian presented a new challenge to us financially, as newborns will: I had to drop out of the work I was doing for the school district to care for him.

The arrival of Christian coincided with that of another visitor, unfamiliar to us and most unwelcome: creditors. We began to fall behind in payments for store credit and other purchases, and bill collectors began to call at odd hours of the day and evening. Nothing in my past prepared me for the anguish that was visited upon us—the sense of humiliation and torment of the constant assaults. At first the callers were cordial, but soon enough they became nasty. Since I was home alone much of the time, I felt particularly vulnerable. Soon enough we learned why many people screened calls—from 1992 till nearly a decade later, I never answered the phone without first finding out who it was. We felt we were under siege.

By early 1993 we'd lost the helicopter, plane, impromptu vacations, and one of our cars—all vestiges of our glamorous life were gone except, a beat-up sedan and our Calabasas property, and the latter was bleeding us to death financially.

In early 1993, desperate to end the anguish, we took our last precious dollars and hired a consultant who accompanied us to a hearing with the Coastal Commission in Eureka, California. Two months later, we got the good news at last: we were free to begin construction!

Practically the same day, our bank statement arrived and showed us we could no longer afford even the mortgage payments, much less the cost of building a new home. A fierce recession was gripping California at that time, and real estate prices were heading downward. We looked into selling the property, but even if we could, we'd only get a fraction of what we'd paid.

For the five years starting in 1988, into the teeth of growing adversity, we were often able to keep ourselves going by imagining what the future held in our new home—the trees, the forest paths, the glorious sunsets radiating across the hills, the gentle ocean breezes blowing our way from Malibu on the far side. And just like that—with the flick of pen—it vanished. We lost not only our dream home, but all the money we'd put into the property from our prosperous years. All gone.

Our tasks, if more grim, at least were more certain: we would make it work in the tiny house in Reseda, get through the lean times somehow, and perhaps a brighter day would one day dawn for us. Greg was getting only about a tenth of the stunt work he had gotten previously, so he did his best to pick up odd jobs and do repairs on cars. During this time, I came to truly appreciate Greg's ingenuity—he was always fixing things, and it became a common refrain among our two boys—"Don't worry, Daddy wick-it!"

He began to answer ads in a local newspaper called the *Recycler*, buying cars cheap (often ones that didn't run at all) and then repairing them and turning them around for a quick sale.

There were challenges. For one, we did not have a tow truck, and to hire one to tow the cars to our house so Greg could fix them would have eaten into our slender profits. We wound up using our aging sedan to tow the cars with cables. We worked it out so that we'd drive together to get the car, then I'd do the towing while Greg remained behind in the disabled vehicle and steered. He also took charge of the braking: when we came to a red light, I had simply to let go of the gas pedal and pray that Greg would push the brakes at the right time and the right pressure to stop both of us. I could not use the brakes in the lead car for fear Greg—towed by flexible cables—would ram into me.

After a while, Greg got out his old motorcycle helmets—with built-in walkie-talkies, that he used for his occasional stunt work—to help in coordinating our driving. It was reassuring to hear his voice tell me he was braking, especially when a busy intersection loomed ahead.

It was a frequent anomaly in those days that often the cars he'd bring home were newer and more expensive than ours, but we never got to keep them. At one point, Greg went to check out a Volkswagen van that looked extremely good—so good he wondered why it was so cheap—till he lifted the hood and discovered it had no engine. He bought it anyway, then watched the papers for two weeks till he found a VW engine for sale, bought it, installed it, and got it up and running. At this point our two sons complained that they wanted to keep it rather than have Greg sell it; I asked them if they wanted to eat. They conceded eating was even more important than a nice VW van, so we sold it and made three thousand dollars.

Because there was little money for toys for the children, Christmas became an acute problem. In Christmas 1993, Joe asked Santa for a new bike, knowing intuitively that while Mommy and Daddy could not afford to buy him one, Santa Claus did not suffer the vagaries of economic uncertainty.

Though of course Santa was every bit subject to those vagaries.

Yet somehow Santa delivered a bright, shiny new bicycle to Joe that Christmas morning. Recently Joe, now twenty-one and aware of how poor we were, asked about that bike. How his Dad and I could have afforded such a luxury?

The answer was simple: Santa had a very skillful elf, Greg, who scoped out the garage sales, and paid five dollars for a rusty, scratched up bike. I thought he was out of his mind, and warned him to dump it lest he disappoint Joe and leave him disillusioned about Santa. St. Nick provided children with a wellspring of hope and a glimpse of a better life in difficult times; the last thing I wanted was for Joe to lose that.

Fortunately Greg ignored my request. He worked on it for weeks, taking it apart completely. He had a metal polisher, and polished each piece of chrome. He sanded all the rusty patches off, and put a glossy red spray paint on it. He cleaned and Amour-all'd the tires. He spent another ten dollars on stickers, a new seat, new rubber handles, and an electronic horn/microphone/siren gismo. It was the coolest bike an eight-year-old could ever want!

When I later explained all that to Joe, he was astonished.

"*No way!*" he said. "That bike was brand new!"

Again, what Greg had accomplished with the bike was a distant echo of what my Grand-Daddy had done those years before with the peach seed monkey.

9. Escape

So we scraped by with hard work and resourcefulness, but even as we did our best to get by, things beyond our control were conspiring to put pressure on our hopes.

By the mid-1990s, the San Fernando Valley had changed from the archetypal suburban utopia as portrayed in film and song—it had become more economically diverse, with pockets troubled by poverty and violence. Further, it was rocked by the Northridge Earthquake (actually centered just a block and a half from our house) in 1994, and was in the grip of the statewide economic downturn that included the closure of a long-operating General Motors plant in the valley community of Van Nuys.

With such stresses on its population, violence was inevitable. Gangs became active across a wide swath of our area. At night we could hear the pop of gunfire and screech of tires as gang bangers raced and chased each other through deserted streets.

The gloom of the world outside our house only intensified the gloom within it as the money vice gripped us tighter. Still, while Greg fought back by picking up odd jobs and getting a day of stunt work here and there, I did my part with what resources I had, learning how to feed a family in lean times. Though I was unable to work because of childcare obligations, that didn't stop me from drawing my very ancient love of games and lifelong experience as a couponer to help us make ends meet.

At holiday time, I would buy three turkeys for $5 each; sometimes, if I played the sales right, I could get them for free. Then I'd freeze two. Each turkey would provide about eighteen meals, with fresh turkey evolving into sandwiches and thence into pot pie. I also learned how to "play" coupons in a winning way. Conventional wisdom has it that it's most economical to buy in bulk, because the unit price goes down. That's generally true—unless you have a coupon, especially one that is doubled in value at a given supermarket. That's because the money saved on a coupon on a smaller item is proportionately more than that on a larger one.

For example, if a 12 ounce bottle of hot sauce sells for $1.99, its price is 17¢ per ounce. Meanwhile, a much smaller 5 ounce bottle might sell for $1.19, or 24¢ per ounce—much pricier per ounce. Now, if you throw in a 50¢ coupon and double it, the bargain is reversed. The 12 ounce bottle sells for 99¢, or 8¢ an ounce—a big improvement. But the smaller 5 ounce bottle will now sell for only 19¢, or 4¢ per ounce—only *half* the price per of the big bottle per ounce! I found that when there are various sizes of the same product, about 90% of the time, this same switch takes place when the coupon is added to the mix.

There were other strategies, too, that had to do more with timing. Our big night out consisted of "99¢ Tuesdays" at Taco Bell— we'd spend $2.97 plus tax on nine tacos—three each for Greg and the boys, and none for me. Inevitably, tacos being what they are, and boys eating the way they eat, lettuce and cheese would fall off their tacos and onto their plates. When they were through, I'd gather all such leavings and make a salad for myself.

100

It was pathetic, but I smiled my way through it, and assured them I actually *preferred* to eat this way. It was, again, a strategy for stretching a little into a lot, and our survival was at stake.

As the months went by I continued to refine my approach, carefully organizing coupons and combining them with sales, and learning how to find unadvertised sales. I also used a strategy of investing. I never made a list of groceries I'd need to make dinner for the week. Instead, I'd look at the groceries I had in the house to determine what I could make out of what I had, then make my shopping list to fill in the blanks, while investing in more good things at great prices for the future. Ultimately, careful shopping grew to be an extra job for me, allowing me to save as much on food as I would have earned working full time at minimum wage.

We had two other resources we leaned on to make ends meet during these days. Furniture was one—we had collected an antique dinner table and other fine furniture, and began to sell it off piece by piece. At least its absence made our small house look bigger. Then there was the Sparklett's jug. During our prosperous Panorama City days we were too busy living the good life to bother with such things as coins, and we had an empty five gallon water jug in the corner into which we'd drop loose change, never giving any thought about what to do with it once it was filled.

When we moved from Panorama City to Reseda, the jug, now three-quarters full, somehow made it with us, and got tucked into a closet, where it was forgotten. As times grew more desperate, I stumbled upon it and got to work rolling coins. The quarters helped feed my family for two and a half months. The dimes took longer to roll, and these lasted only five weeks. The nickels proved to be quite labor-intensive, not only to roll, but also to haul around, and we used them up very rapidly indeed. I can recall ambling up to the counter in the post office on one occasion and handed the lady there $10 worth of nickels.

"Why not use real money?" she asked.

"This *is* the real money," I smiled. "Paper money is just a promissory note. Says so right on the front."

When the nickels were exhausted, we set to work on the pennies, which we rolled and spent over the course of many years.

These measures were enough to keep us going, but not enough to lift us out of poverty. I felt deeply ashamed of our situation. Many afternoons during these days, when I was alone at home with my infant Christian, the doors and windows were closed against the threat of intruders, and the phone had the ringer turned off to keep creditors at bay, I would cry aloud for guidance. I read Psalms, seeking answers. I felt I was drowning, sinking, dying. "I lift up my eyes to the hills— where does my help come from?"

During these moments, I would reassure Christian, who could not yet understand me, that these times would pass. And indeed by early 1996, I believed they would—either we would make the problems go away, or the problems would make me go away. I sought refuge in the church, and in prayer, and when these seemed exhausted, I finally sought refuge in death.

I went to my church constantly to pray to God for guidance and deliverance from the shame of my poverty. I attended a prayer group, and many times shared my tribulations, and sought their prayers and received them. But the prayer group could be a mixed blessing, because even as I asked for answers from God, I felt ashamed in front of the others, and sometimes these others would hurt more than help. It only took one stray comment from someone in the group—"why don't you get another job if you need the money?"—to wound me. As soon as Christian was old enough for day care, I'd been working again—two jobs—and Greg was constantly scrounging for every penny. What more could we do?

At last, in early 1996, after four years of harassment by creditors, I found myself examining the train schedule for Metro North, the commuter rail line in Los Angeles County. I was thinking of escape, not on a train, but beneath one. I memorized the schedule for the times when it crossed Tampa Avenue just north of Parthenia Street, and then, suddenly, on a crystal clear sun washed Monday in February 1996 I told Greg, who was home repairing a car, that I had an errand to run, and commended Christian to his care, and carefully kissed them both goodbye. If they had any sense that my errand would separate me from them forever, they gave no hint of it.

Then I set out for that intersection, my plan carefully worked out. It was to look like an accident. I would pull off on the shoulder and wait till a minute before the train's scheduled arrival, then drive up onto the tracks and cut the engine. I'd keep the doors locked, windows shut, and radio on full blast, so when they found the wreckage, they'd think I'd stalled out and didn't hear the train coming. Before I got hit, I'd duck down on the floor so people would think the car was empty as it sat on the tracks, and take no extraordinary action to intervene.

I arrived at 2:12pm with three minutes to spare, wondering along the way whether I deserved the comfort of air conditioning en route, and deciding that I ought to have it because a normal mom on a normal day doing a normal errand would certainly have it on, because it was hot out, and if it wasn't on when they investigated the wreckage it might raise questions.

My last minutes on earth were to be a comfortable seventy degrees Fahrenheit.

That particular Monday, the train did arrive on time, but just before it did, a violent rain storm hit, with a rip-roaring thunderclap that stirred me to the soul, and the rain from the clouds quickly became rain from my own eyes—a storm of tears. When I opened them, I was no longer at that railroad crossing; I was home—an emotional ruin, whose departure for that appointment had occurred entirely in my mind. It had been a vision, or perhaps an intense daydream, but it had been so vivid I was shaking and in tears afterward. Greg spent the rest of the afternoon comforting me, trying to get from me what it was that made me cry, but I held it inside, and concealed it from him till I wrote this very book.

In the months afterward, I returned many times in my thoughts to that train track, my pain from the indignity of our poverty at times overwhelming not only my desire to spend my life with my husband and children, but also throwing aside any sense I had of how devastated they would be when the inevitable phone call came to the house, and Greg suddenly became a single dad with two young children and little means to support them.

This is to say nothing of the innocent people on the train, whose lives I would have endangered. In the deep well of my despair, such rational thoughts were out of my reach.

Through all this, I spoke not a word of our difficulties to my sister or my father, and I never asked either for help. Why not? Why did I prefer death at the railroad tracks to a simple request for help?

Thinking back on it, I don't know, precisely. Certainly pride played a role; the desperate need we both had to keep our heads held high. I do know that at one point during these difficult days, a member of the church gave us $300 as an outright gift, and we desperately needed it, but I felt perfectly horrible accepting it. I had been involved in charitable activity since a child, so charity was fine with me—as

104

long as I was giving, not receiving. More than once during that time I thought of asking for help from Tree of Life—the ministry for which I was still volunteering weekly to hand out food to the poor. I could have asked when I was packing groceries for others, but never did.

As to my father, I certainly did not feel good about burdening him—I had been independent for almost twenty years, and he had financial challenges of his own. And beyond that, perhaps somehow I did not want him to see me as a failure. I never made a secret of how good things were during our prosperous years, but now that we'd lost it all, the notion of appearing naked—stripped of all the success—before my father and my sister and the rest of my family was more horrifying than death itself.

A bullet finally brought me relief. Not a bullet against me by my own hand, but against our house by a stranger.

One night, as our children were asleep and Greg and I barely awake, we heard the screech of tires outside, and the revving of an engine—no longer uncommon in our formerly quiet suburban street— and also something new—the pop of gunshots as the car drove by. The next day Greg found a bullet hole in the front of the house.

Could we really raise our two children under these circumstances?

We decided to flee.

Our finances were precarious, but we opted to get out of the Valley somehow. The fact that we had a new purpose—a plan to deal with our situation—relieved my depression and got me focused on something positive—and my thoughts of the railroad tracks ceased.

One Saturday morning in August 1996 we drove our car to Simi Valley, a dozen miles northwest of Reseda, on the other side of the Santa Susanna Mountains. It looked like a sanctuary to us, and the rents were reasonable, so it filled us with hope.

The next weekend, we drove to a place called Canyon Country, twenty-two miles to the north. It had the rustic quality that had drawn us to our abortive dream property in the Santa Monica Mountains, though it was less lush, more desert in look and feel.

Unfortunately, there were few rental properties in the area, and none that seemed suitable to our needs. We decided that Simi Valley would be our new home, but somehow the stark beauty of Canyon Country impressed me strongly.

So strongly, in fact, that on a Sunday in early September I decided to take another trip there alone, while Greg was installing a new water pump on a Dodge he bought for $500 and the kids played nearby. I was hoping some rental property would turn up and we'd wind up there.

In fact, nothing was suitable on this trip, either, but as I made my way along Winterdale Road en route to the Antelope Valley Freeway and home, I turned right on a street called Nearview Drive. It was an idyllic suburban byway, enhanced by views of the mountains. One house on the street had a sign in front of it; unfortunately as I drove up I saw it was a FOR SALE, sign, not a rental one.

Still, I felt an unusually strong pull toward the place.

The sign indicated it was a bank repo. I assumed from this that it was empty, and boldly made my way to the front door and peered in through the windows. Even void of furnishings and human occupants, it seemed inviting. I was liking it more.

I made my way around to the rear of the house, and saw that the kitchen window was unlocked, and that the bottom of the window was only as high as the top of the cabinet top. So I slid the window open, and climbed in.

As soon as my feet hit the tile kitchen floor, I knew it was my home.

The view was spectacular. And through all the hard times, that view reminded me of how big God is. The place gave me hope.

But how could we buy it? I wondered. We had assumed we'd be renters the rest of our lives; how could we even entertain the notion of buying a property with our poor credit rating?

For some reason that bleak fact did not deter me. I drove back to Reseda, pulled up in the driveway and asked Greg to get the kids and get in—I wanted to show him our new house. He was perplexed, but went along. We sped back and Greg concurred. We realized when we looked around, and saw a real chance for our children to grow up without the danger of gangs and gunfire, that this was ideal.

But he was just as daunted as I was by the prospect of applying for a loan, ultimately, we simply decided to lay out our situation as it was, our history with all its financial difficulties, and let the chips fall where they may.

Curiously enough, it was indeed something in our history that we had long forgotten about that made a difference: Greg's service in Vietnam. Little good came out of his memories of that time, but one fact followed him from the moment he left: the support of the Veterans' Administration. This agency had a program to help veterans get loans, and they backed us up. The loan was pre-approved just two weeks after I set eyes on what we had already begun describing as "our" house.

Armed with the loan, our realtor put in a bid.

For the next few days, while we awaited word, my thoughts were all on Canyon Country and our new house, and what the move would be like, and how I'd decorate it with such slender resources (I'd be busy sewing curtains again!), and how the adjustment would be for our kids. Such were my thoughts when I came home from work and saw Greg working on a car in the driveway.

He didn't look happy.

Without even looking up, he said, "We didn't get the house." It was clear he was angry and hurt.

I was astonished. "That house was *our* house," I protested.

"No it wasn't," he snapped back. "Somebody out-bid us."

Tears came to my eyes. I was angry and confused. I simply felt we were meant to live in that house.

We stopped actively looking after that. Our funk was deep, reinforced by a physical problem: I needed back and neck surgery in October, and was suffering a painful recovery. The story of how I injured my back was emblematic of the times: a moment of joy sandwiched by misery. In early 1996, my step brother, Steve, died unexpectedly at age 29. Steve was himself a tragic figure—a man who was a true sweetheart, kind to everyone, friends and strangers alike, especially to children. There was not an ounce of malice in him. But he fell into methamphetamine abuse. His father had died of congenital heart failure at a young age, and Steve's use of drugs served to enlarge his own heart. By age 28 he knew he had a year or so to live.

As the end drew near, he was deeply anguished by the fact that he had played a part in corrupting Jimmy, who was then in jail for a third time on drug charges. Upon his death, I learned he had left me shares of a date farm he owned—worth about $600—and his dying wish was that I use it for some joyful purpose, and not for such dreary uses as paying bills.

We cashed in the shares, and while I confess I did not respect his wishes fully—we were desperate, and some bills needed to be paid —we did celebrate. We used some of the money to buy ski tickets for Greg and I up at Mountain High, a public ski area an hour or so from our home. In our prosperous times we had skied often, but we'd long since sold our skis to pay our bills, so it was a real treat.

I long had a habit of challenging myself—of skiing just beyond my ability. In that spirit, all day long I took jumps at the end of a run. As night settled, Greg had had enough.

"Let's head on home," he said.

"One more!" I cried.

"You're wearing out the mountain!" he smiled.

"I can't go yet. We don't know when we'll be back, and I haven't hit this last jump the way I want to."

Greg sighed. "One more."

We hopped on the lift back to the top, and set off at high speed down the run, I pushed myself hard, keeping my speed up higher than I had all day, savoring the sensations of speed and wind. Even Greg had trouble keeping up with me.

As I approached the jump toward the end, I took a steeper angle and focused everything on hitting it just right and tilting my body forward to get maximum time airborne.

Unfortunately I hit it wrong. I'm not sure how; perhaps it was the speed at which I was going—something to which I was not accustomed. For whatever reason, my left foot went too far back as I got airborne, and I tumbled, and landed directly on my head before sprawling several dozen yards to the bottom of the hill..

I instantly knew something was wrong with my back. I went to a chiropractor immediately upon our return. He worked with me for six months, and through it my pain got worse. Gradually my right leg went mostly numb, I developed no feeling in my right hand and a weird pain all down my right arm from my neck. After five months, I suffered flashes of lightning-like pain down my right leg, during which it would collapse momentarily. The pain eventually became so excruciating I couldn't sleep, and at last, after five straight sleepless nights, I visited a medical doctor.

They took X-rays and MRIs, after which I went to see a neurologist. When he entered the examining room, he looked at me curiously.

"I'm sorry," he said. "Wrong patient. I'll be with you shortly."

He went back out and spoke to the receptionist, and asked her where Teri Gault was.

"I'm Teri," I called out.

The doctor came back in, perplexed, looking over the records in his hand. "Then these records are wrong," he said. "These records are for a quadriplegic. If you're Teri Gault you should be in a wheelchair."

We double checked everything and he was stunned. My X-rays and MRI had determined my lumbar region was so badly damaged that I was actually paralyzed from the waist down, with no control over bladder and bowels. It was a miracle I was walking and not wearing diapers.

I was immediately referred for multiple surgeries, starting with my neck, as I was dangerously close to being paralyzed from the waist down. The neurosurgeon told me they had to go through my throat, past the vocal chords, and cautioned that in rare cases patients can wind up with permanent damage or a scratchy voice.

Tears started streaming down my face. He didn't know I was a singer. I was so overwhelmed that I couldn't talk, but Greg was with me and he spoke for me.

"Doctor," he said. "Teri has the most pure soprano voice, and she sings professionally. You can't do that to her vocal chords."

The doctor nodded. "Don't worry. We have another way to go about it."

He flipped over the picture card, and explained that the other way was more invasive: He would go through the back of my neck.

110

"A lot more pain is involved," he said, "and a harder recovery. The trade-off is that instead of going past the vocal chords, we go past the nerves to your right arm. There would be more loss of use of that arm. We can't be sure how extensive—anywhere from minimal to complete loss of the arm forever."

"That's what we want to do," said Greg.

I held Greg and thanked him through sobs. I had no doubt in my mind that I would give up my right arm for my voice. Not a smidgen of doubt. But I was so touched by Greg's resolve on my behalf. He knew full well that if I'd lost complete use of my arm, he would have to do a lot more for me and the kids, but he was ready to make that sacrifice to save my voice, and I was very grateful.

Fortunately, I got through the surgery without extensive additional damage. Recovery was gradual; it took me over a year to get a fair amount of use of my arm back. In the first few months, I dropped things constantly, always shattering glasses and plates. If you have no feeling or reflex, you don't know when something is slipping out of your hand.

Even now, I still have mishaps, but I am able to do most things, including type. I do critical things with my left hand, or I just make sure I focus on using my right hand. I can even play the piano.

In any event, I was recovering from surgery in early November —fearful of how desperate our financial situation was going to look when the full cost of the medical bills—and the work time I lost in recovery, were totaled—when we got a call from the realtor. I didn't even answer it—assuming she just wanted to reconnect with us and try to get us back in the market. As I listened to the answering machine, she told us the house on Nearview had fallen out of escrow.

I was stunned.

This time it was Greg's turn to pull into the driveway, and my turn to deliver the news from our realtor—and this time it was good news.

We quickly made a new bid—somewhat higher—and two days later got word that it was accepted. We closed on our new home in December.

When Reseda was new to us, it was to be a very temporary stop. We were on the brink of building our dream house on dreamy mountain landscape; Joe was just a toddler, and I drove him around in our shiny new Mercedes, and Greg's work and opportunities, and even my own, seemed boundless.

Eight years later, we were a battered family of four, packing up our belongings on what was essentially the wreckage of our sedan, towing a rickety trailer that made us look more like the Joad family from *The Grapes of Wrath* than the up and coming entertainment industry denizens we had once been.

I had become anxious that the growing danger of our deteriorating neighborhood might somehow rise up and ruin our hopes and plans. I wanted to help Greg with the moving as much as possible, but my back surgery had rendered me unable to contribute.

At last, on December 6, 1996, Greg put the car in gear, and we sputtered forward, and waved a few last goodbyes to neighbors, and watched as the Reseda home, and the Reseda years, faded from view.

As we drove out onto Sherman Way toward Interstate 405, I glanced at our gas tank and hoped we had enough gas to make it to our new home. We didn't have any money left to refill it.

10. "Man's Extremity is God's Opportunity"

Canyon Country was a slice of paradise with mountain vistas, quiet streets and safe parks for our children, but our money situation only worsened. Even as we moved in, I became afraid that wouldn't be able to make the payments. But when I walked out to the deck and looked at the view, I felt a peace come over me, as if God was assuring me that we would make it through. I felt more blessed by God's mercy at that moment than at any other time in my life.

Greg continued to repair cars, though there were fewer to be had in Canyon Country, with its sparse population, and when we did find one, we had to tow it a long way. Meanwhile, his stunt work, which had been sporadic, all but died out.

As Christian grew to be a toddler, I was able to get part-time work as a free lancer for a few non-profits, this time doing grant writing. I spent my time researching grant opportunities from various foundations that supported education, and tried to figure out which presented the best "fit" for the needs of various organizations. I then worked with school officials on their priorities—musical instruments, for example, or an after school enrichment program in need of funding—and wrote a grant proposal and submitted it, then waited and prayed. I earned only the minimum wage while researching, writing and submitting the proposals, and when the grant money came through—if it did—I got a commission.

The grants also played directly into my performing arts background, since most were for music and theater. Some of them were even for shows that I would eventually perform in, or work as a teacher.

One day in early summer 1997, Greg pored over the local paper for broken down cars for sale and found nothing promising. But before he threw the paper away, he happened to spot a job for a welder of a gate on a paddock—a small horse corral. I had no idea welding was in his realm of experience, but it turned out he had done it back in Texas, and still had a little portable welding unit for small home jobs, buried among our less-used belongings.

He left that morning and came home with $350 cash, and more: while he had been welding, a neighbor had come up to him and asked him if he'd be available to do another welding job. Within a week, Greg had three more welding jobs, a glimpse at a potentially lucrative money stream—and a big problem. His small kit wasn't appropriate for some of the work he was being asked to do, but a professional kit would cost thousands of dollars.

Fortunately, Greg still had his entertainment industry friends, and even made his way once a month or so to Vito's—which had superseded The Money Tree as a gathering place—to network or, more often these days, to reminisce and reconnect.

Vito's was a colorful dive, a little piece of Brooklyn on Vermont Avenue in a gritty, Bohemian part of Hollywood. It was a great place for Greg emotionally, because it was a place filled with energy, excitement and possibilities. While there were a few stunt people there, it was essentially populated by a colorful group of talkers, young guys and older ones, producers, writers, directors, agents and actors, all of them crowding around small tables, filled with ideas, wheeling and dealing.

One dear friend of ours, Jim Namick, happened to be there the week Greg was wondering what to do about the welding equipment. Jim had been the Production Manager on a lot of Landsburg's movies of the week and other projects, and had hired Greg for a lot of work over the years. The runaway production to Canada had ruined Jim's career in the entertainment industry, and in its place he'd started a metal-spinning business. He often went to auctions and bought big tools and machinery at a fraction of their original cost.

"Why don't you come with me to an auction this Friday?" he asked.

"I don't have much money," said Greg.

"You can get things really cheap," Jim said.

"Tell you the truth, I don't have *any* money."

But Jim insisted he come anyway, and sure enough, on the auction block was a practically new Lincoln *Mig and Tig*, with a wire feeder and hundreds of feet of cable. It was the top of the line welding equipment, worth $7,000.

"I can start the bidding at a dime, but that's my top price," said Greg to Jim.

"If you want it, I'll buy it for you," said Jim. Before Greg could protest, Jim was hot in the bidding, and wound up buying it for $1,800. As soon as he signed the paperwork, he turned it over to Greg.

"But I can't afford it, Jim."

"Don't worry about paying me back," he said. "When you get it, you get it."

Greg took the kit home, and very quickly welding moved the forefront of our income over the repair of automobiles. Sooner than we expected, we were able to pay Jim back.

But Greg paid a high price: Canyon Country was basically a desert land, and temperatures in the summer could climb to 116 degrees. Aside from lifting 150 pound pipes all day, Greg had to wear heavy leather clothing and a protective helmet, and work with intensely hot flame. He was by this time in his late 40s, and it was physically demanding and exhausting work even for someone much younger.

It also proved exhausting for our car. By the middle of 1998, with Greg traveling around Canyon Country doing numerous welding jobs, he began hauling his equipment in the trailer we'd used for our move. The problem is that our sedan, which was never really designed for towing in the first place, was already bone tired from years of hauling broken down cars. Greg sensed that the transmission was about to give, and that we would soon lose our only car.

At that point, we had all of $900 and some change to our name. Greg saw an advertisement for a big truck with a thousand pound lift gate for only $1,800. It was perfect for his needs; the only catch was that the engine wouldn't run.

Greg went to check it out and found a rusted truck that had been parked under a tree for the three years since the owners' husband had died. He made his best pitch to the woman, explaining that all he had was $900, though he conceded to her the truck was worth more that. She relented, and Greg used what spare change was left to hire a tow truck.

So we had a truck that didn't run, and we didn't have a dollar.

"I know what it is—the fuel pump," said Greg. He bought one on credit and began working on the big machine.

As for me: I felt barren, so desperate, more so than I'd felt since the dark days in Reseda. Greg labored through the night and into the next day on the truck, to no avail. I looked over our food supply, and whereas I thought we had three days left, I reworked it and figured I might be able to stretch it to four. I tried not to think about the mortgage payment coming due within the next few days. That night, my father's words of many years ago echoed with me: "The last chapter hasn't been written yet." It gave me a vague hope.

On the second night Greg stumbled up to the bedroom exhausted from staying up almost forty-eight hours straight working on the truck, and collapsed in bed. That night I felt that our house in Canyon County would soon slip from our grasp, as the dream property in Calabasas had done. I played over in my mind what the scene would be like at the bank when we broke the news, except I couldn't see what came next: homelessness for my family? At least when we lost our property in Calabasas, we had our house in Reseda. If we lost the Nearview house, we would truly be destitute.

I was awakened from uneasy sleep early the next morning by the sound of a big, strong, heavy duty engine roaring outside. I ran downstairs to find the truck, with its hood open while Greg stretched out along the side, with one foot on the gas and the other reaching into the engine compartment.

I ran up to him and shouted "My hero!" but he had little time for celebration; he slammed down the hood, threw his tools into the back and got inside.

"Where are you going?" I asked.

"To make some money!" he shouted back as he pulled out.

And so he went to work with his truck, and came back later that day with some cash for me, and I went to work at the supermarket, to make our three day supply of food stretch to a month or more.

Little did I realize as I set out that afternoon, it was a trip that would change my life forever.

117

By this time my shopping and couponing had become so refined that, in a distant echo of my father's game of betting how long it would take a given customer to stand in line at a bank, I played a game to see what percentage of savings I could get out off the normal price of a day's shopping. I'd aim for 50% and gave myself some reward if I managed to beat it. Further, I grew adept at not only taking advantage of sales at the supermarket, but in *anticipating* them, and planning accordingly.

As I stood in the midst of that supermarket that day, I noted a large calendar on the wall announcing a month's worth of sales, and the years of game-playing, coupon-snipping, and mathematical strategizing came together in something of an epiphany. It was a vision, like the one I'd had at the church in Anaheim a few years before. I saw numbers before my eyes; numbers were everywhere; I couldn't stop seeing numbers and patterns. The supermarket seemed filled with mathematics, and at the end of it I realized how I might be able to harness the patterns I was seeing—and had seen for many years —into a systematic approach to saving money that I'd only casually utilized during the course of my life.

The immediate consequence of this vision was that I bought less that day than I'd planned. During the course of the next year, though, I gradually put my ideas to work to generate what came to be known as "Teri's List," and the cost of the food I needed to feed my family dropped tremendously.

Though the true implications of my experience that day were yet more than a year off, the origins of The Grocery Game were born.

By 1998 I was working three jobs—part-time for the school district teaching, part-time writing grant proposals, and part-time performing as an actress, pianist and singer in children's theater for a

118

company called J.P. Nightingale. I was paid $150 for three performance at each school, which usually amounted to a days' work by the time all preparation and breakdown were complete. We toured public schools, especially ones in poor districts as they were more eligible for grant money, and in so doing I was reminded of my own family's poverty. I was working myself to the bone, and so was Greg, but we could not make ends meet. It made no sense to me—while it's true that the cost of living in Southern California is astronomical, somehow the money seemed to vanish as fast as we made it, no matter how much we made.

In June 1999, I finally found out why.

On a furnace-like day that June, 116 degrees in the shade, Greg was working in his full leather welding suit, and was most definitely *not* in the shade. He suddenly felt his muscles seize up, and before he became immobile, he managed to throw his equipment into the truck and drive home. I immediately took him to the doctor, where he was placed on an IV and treated for heat stroke.

He was bedridden for a week, severely dehydrated, with his hands and feet curled up. For a while we feared he would be incapacitated. I tended to him for a few days, and did some of the household chores he usually did, in addition to all my duties and my jobs. In mid-week I got to work on our financial books to pay our bills, which he usually did. He tried to warn me away, but I didn't understand his concern.

Until I saw a statement from one of our credit card companies, which said we owed $40,000, and the minimum payment was $3,000, due within a few days.

I rushed to Greg in the bedroom and told him there was some kind of mistake on the bill, but his eyes told me instantly that it was no mistake. He painfully explained how he'd fallen for a trap—lured by the promise of some "courtesy checks" included in a credit card

119

statement shortly after we bought the house, which he hoped would get us through a particularly rocky time and keep the mortgage payments paid.

Within six months, unknown to me, we had racked up $6,000 in credit card debt and could not pay it off in full, and interest charges began to crush us. We now stood at the brink, with $3,000 due and Greg out of work for at least a week.

Into this gloomy situation, a friend from our Reseda church named Jean paid us an unexpected visit. Jean was a wonderful person who many of my friends believed had the gift of prophecy, but I was in no mood to see anyone. Still, she had come a long way doubtless to check in on Greg, though I wasn't sure how she knew.

"How did you hear about Greg?" I asked when I opened the door for her.

"Hear *what* about Greg?"

She hadn't even known; she had come for a very different reason, and had a strong peace about her.

I explained to her Greg's situation, and she insisted on visiting him and talking to us. I led her upstairs and we found Greg, barely awake, and still suffering.

"I had a vision, I needed to tell you. In person."

"Don't tell me any more bad news, Jean—we've had enough today."

"What bad news? You're going to be wealthy," she said. "I had a vision you're going to be unbelievably wealthy."

Greg and I were not even amused.

"That's very nice of you," I said. "Did your vision tell you when? And how? Maybe within the next few days?"

"No," she said. "But it will happen. You'll be so wealthy some people will be jealous of you."

"We'll forgive them," I smiled.

Jean's visit gave us a real lift—not only her words, but also $200 she insisted on giving us to ease our burden just a bit. We put the money to work paying bills, and put her kind words and her prediction out of mind. Reality was much too insistent for us to ignore, and our situation was driven home the following night, when we had two friends over for a long-standing dinner invitation.

I had felt like canceling it but decided to carry on, despite the fact that Greg would not be joining us—not to mention the precarious state of our finances—because they were good friends who'd had us over to their place many times. To feed them, I had bought something called a "rolled pork roast" at the supermarket, because it was on special and seemed adequate to feed three, with some leftovers for my family.

I had never bought one before, and as soon as I sliced into it in front of my guests, we discovered that the supermarket had packed the inside of the "roll" entirely with lard. My friends laughed, but were shocked when I began to cry. Aside from the unspoken pressure of our debt burden, I had spent precious dollars on the food and now discovered there wasn't enough meat in it for even one meal.

My friends tried to comfort me, and in so doing I disclosed to them how dire our finances were. They replied forcefully that we ought simply to file for bankruptcy.

We'd known other couples who'd gone through bankruptcy, but never seriously considered it. We felt a visceral resistance to it— shame. But as they spoke to me, I could for the first time see it that it offered us a way out. The main advantage was that we could keep our residence even if we lost everything else.

After they left, I discussed it with Greg, and after he expressed the same resistance I'd initially felt, we decided to explore it. It dawned on us that with the anticipated loss now of his welding income, at least for a while, potential homelessness loomed.

It was far simpler than we'd imagined. We contacted a bankruptcy lawyer, who did the paperwork and gave us our bankruptcy filing number.

"What is the number for?" I asked.

"I take it that creditors been calling?" he asked.

"For eight long years."

"Next time one of them calls, just tell them you've filed for bankruptcy and give that number and you will not hear from them again."

I was skeptical, but followed his directions, and discovered that as soon as I gave the callers this information, the nastiness in their voices instantly disappeared and they thanked me for the information in a friendly, polite tone.

We instantly felt a huge burden lifted from our shoulders, and as the calls grew less frequent, a sense of tranquility returned that we hadn't known in almost a decade.

Our bankruptcy filing number corresponded to a date in bankruptcy court, an opportunity for us to plead our case, and for creditors to plead theirs. In the event, only one creditor—Sears, represented by a polite gentleman—showed up, and even he did not testify against us.

And that was that.

The experience left us humbled but now cautiously joyful. We could pay our bills. We could breathe again. We eased our sense of guilt by taking heed of what the bankruptcy lawyer had told us in reviewing our case: when the interest payments we made over the years were totaled, we'd already paid our creditors more than two times the purchase price of the items we'd originally bought.

Still, it was a deeply shameful experience for us, and we kept it hidden from friends and family members alike for many years; in fact, some reading this book will learn about it for the first time.

Looking back on it, I can see that while our filing for bankruptcy marked a low point financially, it was also an important beginning. We didn't know it at the time, but our days of struggle amid scarcity were over. Jean, our spiritually gifted friend, was more right than we could have imagined.

We were on an ascending path once again.

By the summer of 1999, I was trying to minimize driving the sedan as much as possible, fearing it would finally give out altogether. I got permission to borrow a rather old computer from one of the organizations I wrote grants for and brought it home. Between working at home on the computer, caring for Joe and Christian, and spending several hours each week figuring out my grocery shopping plans, I had little time for anything else except sleep, and sometimes there wasn't enough of that.

By then I had highly refined the coupon shopping system that had come to me that singular afternoon in the supermarket the previous year. I had become adept at predicting trends in supermarket sales, and in strategizing the use of coupons. Timing was everything; every week I was able to combine the sales and coupons to get many items for free. Now I was able to save between sixty and eighty percent on grocery bills each week, which was the equivalent of a pay raise of several hundred dollars a month.

Combined with this was the discipline I developed to resist the impulse of shopping based on need. This may sound odd but is in fact central to smart shopping. My strategy was to stock up on items I could get for free or for minimal cost and store them, and skip other items until they went on sale. That might mean going without some basic staples for a week or two, but after I'd mastered the timing, this rarely happened.

For instance, if a particular loaf of bread was on special for 70% off, I would buy a months' supply and freeze what we could not eat in a week, and I would not buy any cold cuts for it that week if none were on sale. The following week, the cold cuts might be 70-80% off with coupons, so I'd buy a months' supply of those, carefully checking expiration dates to make sure they'd last. By playing this delicate balancing game, we always had enough food stocked up, and inconveniences were minimal. It didn't hurt that I'd studied the trends in supermarket sales for years and could anticipate when another staple would be coming up for sale.

By formalizing this in an integrated list, I made the shopping easier not only for me but for friends and family as well. Soon enough, my father, stepmother, sister and lots of friends began to look forward to getting "Teri's List" by email every week, and they benefited accordingly.

In August 1999, Christian came up to me while I was busy clipping and organizing my list for the week.

"What are you doing?" he asked.

"I'm making my list."

"Why?"

"I need it for grocery shopping."

I continued to work sorting, clipping, and compiling. He watched me.

"You look like you're playing a game," he said at last.

"It *is* kind of a game," I told him. "A 'Grocery Game.'"

"Can I play?" he asked. I pulled up a chair and he sat down and started to help me. It became something of a ritual for me and

Christian to play our Grocery Game every Sunday after church services.

On Sunday night, November 7, 1999, I was running late and was just then getting to the List. Joe was already asleep, so I didn't even have the joy of working with him: just the prospect of several hours of work, late into the night. I was sitting at the computer, looking totally stressed, when Greg asked me what was wrong.

"It takes ten to fifteen hours each week to come up with the grocery list. I wish someone would make the list and I could just get it and go shopping."

Greg asked me what it is, exactly, that I did that saved so much money. I told him the short version.

He was quiet for a minute or so, then he said, "You should sell it to others."

"What others?" I said. "My dad? Sister?"

"No, customers," he said.

"What customers?" I asked.

He thought about it for a moment longer. "On the Internet. It strikes me as an Internet business, and if you had enough customers, it could be your job and you wouldn't need to hold any others."

I told him I would think about it, then went back to work. The next day, Greg came back to me with the name of a web site and said that he knew I didn't have any experience on the Internet, but that he thought I could handle it.

11. The Grocery Game

It was a modest yet daring proposition: if our family, friends and relatives could use my list to save money, maybe other families would be interested—and willing to pay for it. I was doing the work anyway; why not sell the list—for a modest price? And if I could use the Internet to deliver it to customers, I could save the cost of postage and ensure instant delivery.

There were some problems, though. One was my nearly complete ignorance of the Internet. The other, as usual, was money: inevitably there would be startup and marketing costs.

Greg's discovery of the Internet offer helped solve the first problem. It was for renting web space from a Nevada web hosting and design company at $39.95 a month for a two year contract, with the first three months free.

"A two year contract?" I asked. "Can we really commit to that?" I quickly calculated that we would be committing ourselves to almost $900 over the next two years.

We mulled it over for the better part of a day, and researched it as best we could, and were not able to find any better deal. In the end we were back where we started—unsure.

"We don't get any customers, we simply cancel, and see what happens," said Greg.

"If they'll let us," I said.

By day's end, we decided to go forward.

I quickly learned the ways of web design from the simple tools the web site offered, and within a week, *TerisShoppingList.com* was born. We listed the service as available for $20 for twelve weeks, $32 for twenty-four weeks and $49 for a year, and also offered a free trial.

And then we waited.

As we debated the means of publicizing our site, we got a check in the mail—$49 for a full year. We were shocked.

And also afraid to cash the check.

"What if no one else signs up?" I asked Greg. "We're stuck doing all the work for one person for a whole year. Just the cost of the web hosting service would have been $400."

Yet we desperately needed the money.

We resisted the impulse to cash it, and held on for another week. We were ready to return the check on the eighth day, when two more checks came in the mail. We promptly cashed all three.

The game was on!

Our next big task was marketing. Greg felt that if we could get two thousand members, we would be grossing close to $100,000 a year, and would be set. Three people had stumbled onto our web site; how could we expand our exposure? We knew nothing about web links, search engine positioning and other marketing techniques of the World Wide Web; the internet was fairly new and we were of course new to it. We were still thinking in analogue terms, and that's how we began our task: instead of using pixels transmitted by the megabyte over wires, we made up flyers using ink, paper at the local Kinko's, transmitted them by foot and placed them on the windshields of cars parked in supermarket parking lots.

Greg would take the flyers by the thousands in his truck, and distribute them every spare minute he had, on the way to and from welding jobs, on any errand he might run. Sometimes, when he had no welding jobs, nor car repairs pending, he would simply camp out in a supermarket parking lot all day and put the flyers on windshields at intervals, ensuring that everyone who'd shopped there that day got word of our company.

During the course of the first two months, orders began to trickle in.

Meanwhile, the web site was having its own "teething" problems, especially with the web address TerisShoppingList.com. When typing the name into their browsers, people often omitted one of the *s*'s between *Teri's* and *Shopping*. People also had a tendency to put in apostrophes where none were needed. And they would spell the name wrong.

As time went on, I compiled the errors and started buying up all the domain names with alternative spellings, but there was a limit to that. Sometimes customers would reach me and tell me things like "A friend told me about you but I could never find you. I searched for Lori's List and Shari's List and got nowhere. I just couldn't remember your name was Teri."

How could I buy up all the web addresses with various women's names with two syllables, even if we could afford it? We were losing an unknown number of customers for very trivial reasons. We needed a new approach.

My son Christian gave it to me. "Since it's the Grocery Game, why not call it that?" he said one Sunday morning as I was busy at work on the week's list.

I had always loved alliteration. And in addition to my son Christian, many of my customers and friends had already told me it was very much like a game. I typed in the web address *www.TheGroceryGame.com* and to my astonishment, it was not taken. I quickly bought it up and The Grocery Game as a web presence was born. The next day, February 8, 2000, I rolled the last of the pennies we had in the Sparklette's water jug and used the money to buy my business license. We were official.

Six months after we launched our business, we had about 350 members, generating around $1,300 per month in gross revenue. It had taken a lot of flyers to get those results, but we were pleased and seemed to be on our way.

We still had some lessons to learn, as we soon found out.

The first Friday of May 2000, I compiled my list and logged onto the web site to update it, and encountered a rather odd message: THE PAGE CANNOT BE DISPLAYED. I tried retyping the web address, and got the same result. I waited a while, then retried—same. I showed Greg. We started to get worried. We called the toll-free number of the web hosting company and it rang for a long time before an answering machine picked up.

It wasn't the standard greeting. It was the voice of a woman, who sounded like she was trembling, and, possibly, crying.

She whispered: "This company is no more. They don't know I'm leaving this message. Cancel your credit card. Take the matter into your own hands. They don't know I am telling you this. Call the police."

It was bone chilling. Our credit card was indeed still being charged, by a company that was obviously no longer in business. I cancelled our credit card and called the Las Vegas police to tell them what was going on. They took the information but we never heard from them again.

I kept trying the site, hoping it would appear. I had no understanding of where it went; I kept picturing my web site floating out there in space. It had taken me a full week of tedious work to build it myself, and I wanted it back. Not only that, I had those 350 paid customers to service, and the new list was to go live the next day.

Fortunately, I had everyone's email addresses, so I put my list in a Word document and emailed it from my Yahoo email address. Even this proved difficult, because Yahoo limited users to emailing only fifty emails per hour. I was up all night and through the next day emailing my clients the list.

As soon as that task was done, I found another web hosting company and spent the next three weeks building a new web site from scratch, while continuing to use email to send out the list to my customers.

With the web problems cleared up—at least for the time being—we continued to plow ahead with marketing. All during the hot summer of 2000, Greg spent every spare moment staking out supermarkets and putting flyers on windshields. Meanwhile, I was writing up press releases and sending them to local media outlets, hoping to get good publicity. This was the heyday of the "dotcom" explosion, so stories about innovative startups were common. Unfortunately, no one seemed interested in *our* dotcom.

Greg's hard work gradually paid off. It seemed that for every thousand flyers, we would get one or two customers. By November

2000, one year after we launched the internet site, our customer base numbered 450.

During 2001, I continued to work on The Grocery Game, did grant proposal writing for the public schools, performed for the J.P. Nightingale children's show, and raised two children, while Greg continued to work hard in the welding business. Our list was growing, and income was getting better, and by November, our member base numbered 1,200. We were prospering again—not the explosive prosperity we'd known in the eighties, but we were able to make ends meet, pay our bills, and save a little. But I found that managing the business was taking more and more time, and I was in a constant state of exhaustion. I longed to soar but felt earthbound by the obligations I had to my other jobs.

On November 9, 2001, our family became airborne at last—a very different kind of airborne than we'd known with our aircraft two decades before. That day, I loaded the computer equipment into our new van (we had sold the sedan at long last), and drove to the office of one of the last organizations for which I wrote grants. It was my last day on that day job, and I was returning the tools of my trade: computer and printer, borrowed two years earlier. I was treated to an impromptu going away party at a local restaurant, then said my goodbyes. I felt a huge sense of relief, like I was making it across the finish line.

I resigned from J.P. Nightingale shortly thereafter, and once again, performing as an actress disappeared from my life.

Free of these encumbrances, I redoubled my publicity efforts. For this I drew on my considerable experience writing grant proposals, which included writing press releases. I also read books to polish up my approach.

Despite my efforts, it was not until just after New Year's, 2003, that I hit pay dirt. In October 2002, I'd left a voice message with reporter/producer Joyce Huntington of KNBC in Los Angeles. In January, she finally returned my call, and said she'd used the password I'd provided her for the web site, and had been using The List for a few months already, and was impressed.

She came to my house two weeks later, and after an hour long interview, we headed out to a supermarket to do a shopping trip, and afterward went to another member's house to interview her.

Here I found that my acting experience helped me to feel relaxed in front of the camera. Back in my acting days, in order to keep myself from being nervous on interviews, I would often ask the interviewers about themselves, or ask their opinion about the script. Nothing technical, just engaging them on a personal level.

So when Joyce came to my house, I chatted with her about where she lived, and asked about her family, and her professional life. Once I'd connected personally and the camera began to role, I naturally felt comfortable. When we were through, Joyce thanked me for a very positive experience, and the segment aired a month later— during sweeps. I suppose it's not entirely true that the last television role I played was a mother in *Days of Our Lives* in 1985. In February 2003, I played an entrepreneur who'd started a rising company that made its money helping families to feed themselves.

My appearance on KNBC was the first of what became a flood of interviews during the next two years. I knew in my heart that we were a good story, the kind of news story they'd like to find. I often hear that we are the highest rated story for many television stations; I had a producer from Fox Los Angeles call me in 2005. I had been on his show in July 21, 2003, and he told me that to date we were the highest rated piece the station has ever had.

In mid-2002, while I continued to work the business, Greg's "big idea" friends at Vito's started urging him to formalize the business by incorporating it. Greg and I were also starting to think bigger—could we expand beyond the local market? After all, the internet reached across the globe, and we were only doing business in our own backyard.

The chief obstacle to a wider reach was that I'd have to travel to other localities to draw up Lists related to those regions—a process prohibitively time consuming and exhausting.

The thought occurred to us that we might be able to franchise the business—in effect, having people in various localities gather data and draw up lists, giving us the ability to provide Teri's Lists across the country. We took this idea to a major law firm in a glass and steel high rise in Century City, where a lawyer listened to us patiently, then told us that if it could be done at all, the estimated legal fees would be $70,000-$100,000 or more.

We were floored. We were *grossing* that in a full year; how could we afford that much—when we weren't even sure a franchise approach would turn a profit?

We went home discouraged, and I continued to work the List and Greg continued to supplement the income with welding and other odd jobs. He also commiserated with his friends at Vito's, where a producer friend recommended he contact a Beverly Hills attorney and literary agent named Richard Herman to see if he might be of help.

We made an appointment with Richard the following week and discovered a well-dressed and friendly man in an office cluttered with screenplays, contracts and deal memos. Unlike the sterile offices of the attorney we'd tried before, Richard's looked comfortable, lived in and appropriate for a very creative person.

We explained to him our business and our situation. Richard was a bit out of role, as he was used to hearing pitches for screenplays from writers, and in turn pitching screenplays to studios and production companies. In a sense, though, he was right at home with us, because we *were* pitching—in this case, not a story idea but a concept for a nationwide company. And just as in fielding pitches for stories, Richard was always thinking in terms of the mass market, and thus he was really right at home in hearing us out.

The first thing you have to do when you pitch a story idea is to whet the agent's appetite and make him or her want to hear more. As soon as I began to speak, he picked up on my passion for The Grocery Game, and instantly responded to its potential. We'd passed the first test: he did want to hear more, and we set up a subsequent meeting, before which he told us he would do more research into franchising—first with an eye to discovering whether or not The Grocery Game was even *franchisable,* and if it was, how much legal work would indeed be involved.

The following week we saw him again, with high expectation and some trepidation, too. In characteristic style, he laid everything out on the table: he felt our business was franchisable, but that it would be complicated to expand the business across the country in this manner.

We braced ourselves for the final blow to our hopes—that he would require a substantial fee. Here, he offered a deal instead: he would undertake the work involved in exchange for a stake in the company. He was impressed enough with our concept that he was willing to invest his time in it to see it grow. We excitedly agreed to his terms, on the spot.

12. Taking Off: The Sequel

We were in for a bit of a shock as soon as Richard came on board. In a word, he was *transformational*.

He immediately threw himself into the task of changing what was literally a Mom and Pop operation into a formidable company. His energy and enthusiasm pushed us forward not only legally but also in sales and marketing. Within a short time there was a huge map of the United States on his office wall to help him visualize what he hoped would be a rapid nationwide expansion.

He soon urged us to hire a public relations firm in New York, a company that could coordinate print, radio and television mentions and appearances and give us a significant amount of promotion. He explained that in order to be successful, The Grocery Game needed a nationwide presence, and that to interest franchisees, it needed to be perceived as a substantial, rock-solid nationally known company. It had to shed its mom and pop image, and fast.

In October, I got a call from Richard: "Pack your stuff—we're heading to New York City."

I was thrilled about going to New York—I'd been there briefly in our prosperous years, as a singer in a chorus on *Good Morning*

America, but that had been long ago, And I was sold on the idea of hiring a public relations firm—depending, of course, on the cost.

It proved an exhausting, exhilarating—and very *cold*—experience. I was an inveterate California girl, and even the winters I vaguely remember growing up in Oklahoma scarcely prepared me for the frigid blasts we endured walking on New York's fabled sidewalks.

Richard had scheduled a series of meetings with a half-dozen of the best public relations firms, and for once someone *else* was doing the pitching to *us*. We listened as each explained why their particular firm was just right for our purposes. On our second last day, we visited one more company—Lippe Taylor, on Park Avenue South. They were pricey, but their presentation seemed the most thoughtful and cogent.

Afterward, we made our way up to a little café at Avenue of the Americas and Central Park South, near our hotel. Here, we tried to share impressions and thoughts about the firms we'd interviewed.

Without reaching a conclusion, we bundled up against the cold and made our way out to the sidewalk, and crossed Avenue of the Americas. As we did so, I glanced downtown, and was stunned. It was devastatingly familiar.

I saw the canyons formed by the huge buildings, receding as far as the eye could see, disappearing into distant fog. The windows twinkled, and at a glance they seemed to form a river of light, that flowed down into the headlights of the thousands of cars and taxis rolling uptown to meet us. And I saw multitudes of pedestrians on the sidewalks.

It was the vision I'd seen during church service in Anaheim, thirteen long years before. I continued to stare till the signal light changed. Richard and Greg, who'd continued to walk onward, rushed back out into the middle of the street to rescue me from oncoming traffic.

I mulled over the meaning of this sudden reappearance of that vision that night and during the next day of sightseeing. It certainly seemed to confirm that this journey to New York, and with it our hopes to build a national presence—was meant to be.

There remained the question of which firm to choose. That evening, over dinner at the Stage Deli, we agreed on Lippe Taylor.

By November 2002, Greg and I were enjoying our upward trajectory. Our lives were the mirror opposite of what we'd known from 1988 through 1999, the long, long years of decline. Everything that was going wrong then seemed to be going right now; the wrong decisions we made and wrong turns we took in the Reseda Years suddenly became the right ones.

They say, though, that if you want to make God laugh, just tell him your plans. That month, I was visited by an old acquaintance that posed a significant threat to everything we'd built: a life-threatening case of pancreatitis. Apparently I inherited the gene that killed my mother.

On a quiet Saturday afternoon in November 2002, I began to feel pressure and agitation in my abdomen. Eventually, it turned into a lot of pain. My first thought was food poisoning; by that night, I was vomiting. All night long I thought, *I'm going to die.* Yet pancreatitis never occurred to me, which was odd, because these were the symptoms my mother always had.

By morning, Greg took my blood pressure, and it was alarmingly low.

"I'll take you to the hospital," he said. "Just let me brush my teeth."

"There's no time," I said, literally feeling my life ebbing.

He immediately called 911.

As I was carried out of the house on a stretcher I could see, somehow, in the trees beside the house, a vision of paradise that is difficult to describe. There was a warm glow, like a sunrise coming from just beyond the trees, lighting them up in a way that made their upper branches look like they were on fire. And there was a sweetness to the way the trees glowed and swayed, and the light shone behind them, and it drew me to them.

I recognized that I was near death. Twice in her own life, during bouts of pancreatitis, my mother had been clinically dead, and revived, and on both occasions she later told me about the light, and the sweetness of it, and how hard it was to keep herself from it.

So it was for me: it took my every effort to remain conscious and fight the impulse to surrender. I found myself quietly praying to God to let me live to raise my children. That was all I asked for.

My prayers were answered.

After three weeks in the intensive care unit fighting for my life, I was allowed home to recuperate. Even then, things did not get back to normal. I was fed only by I.V., no food or water by mouth, not even ice chips. I was assigned a nurse to come by to change my I.V. twice a day, for four weeks.

At one point, I thought, *If I could only have one thing, either food or water the rest of my life, I would choose water.* I was so very thirsty. Yet, when I was tested with an ounce of water, my body went into massive dysfunction. After two months, the doctors explained to me that I was reaching a point where my organs would begin to shut down if I was not able to eat or drink through my mouth.

During those days, I looked again at the Psalms that had guided me through my other times of trial, and came across the 128th, which read in its sixth verse—"may you live to see your children's children"—and I hoped the Lord would extend my fervent request that I live to raise my children to include my grandchildren as well.

Finally, in the fifth week, I was able to drink, and could eat food a week thereafter, and I was on the road to recovery.

The night of December 6, 2002, when I was resting at home and doing much better, I came to a momentous decision. I reviewed our finances carefully, and my workload, and decided I had an opening for a Chief Financial Officer. When Greg got home from doing his welding, I asked him to come into my office, and told him about the opening. We had an impromptu "interview"—more reminiscent of the casting couch experience than anything appropriately corporate—and afterward I told him he was hired for the job.

Things were truly changing, and for the better.

Greg would weld no more forever.

It seemed to me that my path was now clear—I'd be able to be both a stay-at-home Mom, and still run a very successful business. As it had been so many times previously in my life, though, the way things worked out was not quite as I'd planned.

In February 2003, Richard sold our first franchises, just as Lippe Taylor got to work scheduling media appearances for me across the country. I found myself traveling more often than I had since Greg's boom days of stunt work in 1985, and making more television appearances than I had in my entire television career. I was most definitely *not* a stay-at-home Mom. Fortunately, Greg was working from home and could take care of the kids, and loved every minute of it.

The nationwide appearances in print and television media made marketing the franchises much easier, and Richard was able to sell four more in rapid succession.

By mid-2003 I was traveling as often as possible with my sister Karen, who was working part-time as a bookkeeper for a construction company. It helped tremendously to have her moral support during those long, grueling airplane rides, punctuated by a frantic stop and interview with a local news outlet.

The extra nationwide publicity led to more franchise sales. The map on Richard's wall was becoming more and more populated with pins marking the regions where we had Lists; it started to look like an army based in Southern California marching its way across the United States! By mid-year we were up to over ten thousand customers.

The explosion in the customer base brought us problems with our web hosting service—we were constantly overloading it and causing it to crash. As a result, we purchased our own servers, and now have a dynamic web site with custom software.

Our business had become a triumph; no other word fits. The distance we'd come in just a few years was underscored when we got a call from none other than Jim Namick, who'd so generously purchased the professional welding equipment for Greg back in 1997. It seemed his metal spinning company was foundering and he was in trouble. We promptly made financial arrangements to see him through. We considered it a big blessing to be in a position to pay him back for the generosity he had shown us during our lean years.

At this point, with Joe a young adult and Christian ten years old, we decided it was time to expand once more—this time domestically. It came time to take leave of our house on Nearview that had been our salvation from our darkest days. We began going out almost every Sunday, sometimes with a realtor, and sometimes on open houses, to explore our options. We looked in Canyon Country, under circumstances far more favorable than in 1996. But we took our time; gone was the desperation of our flight from Reseda.

By the spring of 2004, our member base had exploded to close to 20,000, and the revenue stream opened up many more options to us in terms of price. We narrowed down our search to the Sand Canyon neighborhood, an idyllic stretch with rolling hills nestled hard by Oak Springs Canyon Creek.   My imagination soared when I visited the neighborhood, and hoped to move there by April.

Unfortunately, Greg's father passed away March 30, and we became preoccupied with those issues of loss, and I bore no further thought of moving in the months that followed.

Then, abruptly in late May, Greg said after church, "You want to go to some open houses?"

We quickly checked the paper and saw an ad for an open house in Sand Canyon, and got in the truck. As we were heading up the street, we saw an open house sign for a different house, and decided to stop.

This time I walked in the front door—rather than sneaking in through a window in the back—and saw the realtor standing at the dinette table in the kitchen. I walked straight over and shook her hand, and felt myself really drawn to the back yard.

"I'd like to see the backyard first," I said. Perhaps that *was* a distant echo of my first experience on Nearview, when of necessity I saw the backyard before getting inside.

"Go right on through," she replied, smiling.

I walked down to the creek that wound its way around large, shady trees, and instantly I thought of a Psalm that I'd read hundreds of times during our trials that spoke of flood, of raging waters that threatened to sweep us away. I had felt ensnared and trapped, now felt delivered from being drowned. I was on the other side of the flood. Greg came out, and I turned to him.

"This is my house."

"You haven't even seen the house," he laughed.

"I don't care."

We soon made an offer, and set a closing date of August 10, 2004

As that date drew near, our excitement grew, but one complication intervened: Lippe Taylor had scheduled me for a publicity trip to New York City during that week. Greg would have to manage the closing and move without me.

When I called anxiously the evening of August 10, Greg assured me everything had gone well. Then he added one tidbit:

"I got you a little surprise."

I tried in vain to draw him out on what that surprise was, but I had a suspicion.

For the early part of my life, there was always a piano in the house. The one I grew up with was a humble affair called a Betsy Ross spinet, a compact upright piano with a loose action and a bright tone. I was used to it and its quirks and I loved it.

Unfortunately, it was destroyed in the fire in December 1973. I really mourned the loss of that piano, and its tone and how the keys felt to me. It was a loss that was never replaced.

When we got married, I didn't have a piano. One day, Greg caught me crying about it, so he went out and bought me a used upright and surprised me with it. I tried to like it, but instantly knew I would play it only rarely. He could tell I was not happy, and wanted to know why.

"The sound," I said. "It's just not like my old Betsy Ross." I knew I would get no joy out of playing it. And it quickly went out of tune.

He felt bad, and insisted we go out to Owen Piano in Canoga Park, where they featured a large stock of used pianos. I was looking at some that were between $500 and $1,000. Greg found one made by Kawai and had me play it; it sounded like my Betsy Ross, and I fell in love with it.

Unfortunately the price got in the way: $2,400. I walked away from it and moved on, despite Greg's protestations and insistence that he buy it for me. I loved that piano—the action and the tone. It was a console, like my old Betsy Ross. During the years that followed, I learned to love Kawai pianos. They are all hand made, in the old way, and Greg always told me he wanted me to have a grand Kawai some day.

Our new house even had a space for a grand piano—the sellers had one and it greatly enhanced our sense of the interior.

So when I got home, it was not much of a surprise—but it was wonderful nonetheless. I'd waited twenty-one years from the moment I spotted the Kawai in the showroom, and thirty-one years from the fire that took my Betsy Ross. Greg had bought me a Kawai grand.

I felt a tinge of worry about the expense; even though we were doing very well, I was reluctant to spend that sort of money. But Greg was my Chief Financial Officer, and he assured me it would be all right.

He was right. By the end of the year 2004, our business had truly expanded nationwide, and what had begun in 1999 with one member and a slender $49 check had now, five years later, blossomed to over 23,000 members. By early 2006, our member base stood at 60,000, and by my calculation, as many as 250,000 people—the families and friends of those members—were benefiting from Teri's List, eating better and living better because of the work we were doing.

13. The Journey

On June 2, 2005, my father joined my mother in Heaven. His wonderful voice, that had filled so many churches and halls, was stilled at last by cancer that took him far too soon. He is in a much better place now; I know it.

My brother Jimmy's life continued on its troubled way after we put him up at our house in the early 1990s. He was busted in 2000 and convicted of dealing methamphetamines and has spent the last five years in prison. Somewhat miraculously, the judge allowed him to leave prison long enough to attend my father's funeral. He was released from prison in December 2005 and seems genuinely changed, and ready to take responsibility for his life.

My sister Karen remains my pillar of strength, working for me and with me on the business; I trust her utterly and am so very grateful she remains in my life on a daily basis.

Somehow I feel that my own last chapter is being written now, and it seems a good one. Our prophetic friend Jean, who'd seen a bright future for us during some very dark days, had been more correct than we could have imagined.

As I write this, it is late afternoon, and a warm desert breeze stirs the branches of the trees in the backyard above the winding stream, and I'm reminded of the desert winds of the Promised Land in ancient times.

In Altus, the sun has already set and, though doubtless a gentle quiet is settling on the town, my father's voice still echoes in the many recordings he made of sacred songs, still played there. In Anaheim, the home I spent my teenage years belongs to another family now. There, a cool ocean breeze is probably urging teenagers home from the beach for dinner. The Love Shack is long gone; a housing tract has replaced it, and where grass sprouted through our kitchen floor, young families have sprouted and are making their uncertain ways in the world, as we did once. Reseda seems the most distant to me now, far in miles, far in days. A safe distance away.

But the trials of Reseda are what forced us to be resourceful, and that resourcefulness finally gave birth to The Grocery Game. I think sometimes about those great trees in Sequoia I saw many years ago, born from ashes, and I think about this journey that Greg and I have been on. We mourned. We were burned to ashes. And from those ashes something very good has flowered and prospered. I never would have started The Grocery Game if we had not been stripped down to nothing, down to ashes.

And now as I meditate on our success, I feel good, because we succeeded by helping families. This finally is the true meaning of that vision I had way back in 1988, the vision in which I fed people whose faces I could not see. I had long been perplexed by that detail. The reason became vividly clear to me just a short time ago, when a woman emailed that she had been left with three kids and only $38. She told me that she couldn't have made it without The Grocery Game, and I felt so touched that I wished right then that I could see her and her children. I was helping to feed them, but couldn't see their faces, because of the technology of the internet—they were only names and email addresses, they were "hits" on our web page, but each of those hits came from a family whose hunger we were helping to satisfy. Now I know who those faceless people are that I was feeding in my vision.

Since then, many have written to me and told me how much TheGroceryGame.com has helped them, and they are fully human to me, and I can identify with them all the more because their struggles to keep food in the house were once our own. And our story has brought hope to a lot of people who have come to know us.

My prayers for a return to prosperity were answered, but even as I look out now on the things we have, I know that the Peach Seed Monkey is still in my possession, safe in its cotton-cushioned box, tucked away in a quiet corner of the house. I gave it to my son Joe, but he asked me to keep it till he is more settled in life, and I have done so. In all our material wealth, it remains our most valued possession.

14. Teri's Top 10 Grocery Saving Tips

I call it a game for many reasons, but one of them is that "couponing" can be fun, and very productive when you know "how, when, where, and what" to buy. The exhilaration of "winning" at the register has often been compared to hitting the jackpot in Vegas!

Player of TheGroceryGame.com benefit from our market research and receive a weekly compiled and integrated list of which items will be on sale the following week, which coupons will be available for them, and therefore the total savings available per item. However, everyone can benefit by some of the principles we urge our players to follow in doing their shopping.

These principles, simple shopping tips, may surprise you, because they actually contradict what many "coupon Queens and Kings" have advocated for decades. Nonetheless, this is what works for thousands of members at TheGroceryGame.com. While this is only part of what is offered to members of *The Grocery Game*, these "Top 10 Tips" should turn your thinking around, as well as your grocery budget!

Each tip, on its own, may not have a significant impact. But when you add them all up, you have a conceptual understanding of The Grocery Game, and you should become a winner at the market.

1. *Investing* vs. *Need Shopping*. Contrary to what your frugal instincts may tell you, you should buy *more* than you "need" to save the most! Crazy? Certainly not! Every item you buy at the market falls into one of these two categories: *Investing* or *Need Shopping*. Even though you don't yet "need" it, if it is an item that is at a *Rock Bottom Sale*, and you have a good coupon to go along with it, and it is something your family may use, you should stockpile it; you should buy it *now*, even though you don't yet need it.

On the other hand, if you don't have it in your stockpile, and you need it today, you may buy it as a *need* item. This will cost you more, but as you continue to shop smart, your *need* list will get shorter and your stockpile will grow, and you will have to do less need shopping.

2. Two Different Supermarkets. Usually, if you have more than one supermarket in your area, one of them will be better for investing and the other for need shopping. If you have a market that doubles coupons, that market will be your *Investing Market.* Whether or not you have a market that doubles coupons, your Investing Market will most likely be a market with higher over-all prices.

Surprised? Yes, participants in the Grocery Game usually "Invest" at the market with the highest over-all prices. That's because they will probably bottom out lower than the other markets, when they offer their *Rock Bottom Sales*. We do not buy their regularly priced items, but we do benefit from their Rock Bottom Sales, combined with a coupon. As for Need Shopping, we go to what I call the *cardboard box* market: a market with no frills, just the lowest prices. And that market typically will not double coupons. Some may not even accept coupons.

3. The Grocery Hopper. Is that you? Do you go to a number of markets to cash in on the best deals each week? I used to say that wasn't productive. But marketing has changed, and this activity, otherwise known as "Cherry Picking" can be time consuming, but profitable. It's time-consuming, because of comparing various sales circulars and coupon match up sites, and honing in on the best price for each item. TheGroceryGame.com is the only place on the web where you can combine all the best deals from numerous stores in one comparative matrix. Plus you get the advantage of advertised sales, which often make up over sixty percent of the deals. Now, cherry picking is easy, fast, and even more profitable.

4. *Rock Bottom Sales* vs. *Phantom Sales* and *Sales Cycles*. Just because an item is on sale and you have a coupon doesn't mean it is time to use the coupon. In fact, most often it is the wrong time! Lurking on every aisle and in every ad are the dreaded *Phantom Sales*, sales that do not offer the supermarket's lowest prices for those particular items. Nearly every item from every manufacturer runs through several Phantom Sales before it reaches a true Rock Bottom Sale.

This is where knowing when to stockpile with that coupon can save you loads of dough at the check out! Begin to keep track of how often each item cycles through its Rock Bottom Sales and Phantom Sales. How much is that item when it is at Rock Bottom? There are a number of ways to track sales cycles. The most obvious way is just to have a "conceptual awareness" of the cycles. Another way is to build an actual database. (At TheGroceryGame.com, members access Teri's List, which takes care of all that database research on a weekly basis).

5. Categorical Sales Trends. Did you ever notice themes within supermarket sales campaigns? One week they may feature paper goods and deli products, another week, sales might be on frozen foods, and toiletries, and nothing else. That's because sales trends run in categories in the supermarkets.

Outside of investing, you are never going to get everything you need at a great price in any given week. In fact, if you don't stockpile properly, you will be forced to overpay on more categories than you are saving on. And it is set up that way for a reason! The categorical sales trends typically cycle through all the categories within a twelve-week period. So stockpile more than you need while the price is right.

6. The Coupon File. Less is more! Forget those big boxes. Toss them! And toss out those old coupons that you will never use, the ones that are for very little money off, the ones you know will never amount to good enough savings compared to generic brands.

Use a simple cancelled check file to organize your few, select coupons. Get your coupons from the Sunday paper *only*. Most other sources for coupons are sub-standard—they are for less money off. My slogan is "Don't litter your coupon file!" Filling your file with substandard coupons makes more to cut, more to file, and more to look through, without delivering more savings! Who needs that?

7. Coupon Redemption. Be careful to read everything on the coupon. You don't want surprises at the check out. Also, look for words like "good on any…" especially when a specific item is featured in the picture. Often times, you may use the coupon on "any" of that manufacturer's products, not just the pictured item.

8. Shopping Days and 72-hour sales - Shop on Sunday, Monday, and Tuesday for most markets. Most markets' sales weeks begin on Wednesday and end on Tuesday. But since you get new coupons to go with the current week's sales on Sunday, wait until then to shop. Also, from time to time, most markets run special 72-hour sales. And most often those sales are Sunday through Tuesday. For sales weeks that begin on Sunday and end on Saturday, you have even more time to shop!

9. Smaller Package = Better Value. Do the math. Most often, when a smaller package and a larger package of the same name brand product are both on sale, the better deal is the smaller package, if you have a coupon to go with it. Yes, that's right! More often than not, a coupon has more impact against a smaller package. Get your calculator to prove it!

10. Warehouse Club Stores. If you have a market that has great rock bottom sales (and most do), you should easily be able to beat "Warehouse Club Store" prices by using your coupons at your Investing Market with a Rock Bottom Sale and applying all the principals of The Grocery Game.

15. Living Gracefully: Other Practical, Money Saving Tips

Through the various ups and downs of my life, and through the launching of The Grocery Game, I have prided myself in being able to make fun out of what I was doing, whether or not we had material things, and whether or not the activity at hand was something that lends itself to fun.

I have also prided myself in having a down home, practical, common-sense approach to everyday situations, and solving them in a fun, playful way. I make it a habit of posting these "Teri's Tips" on my blog at TheGroceryGame.com, but below I'll share a few. Like The Grocery Game itself, these do not require any significant financial or material investment; they are simply a way of arranging your world in a way that makes more sense; living gracefully, if you will.

Hang Damp Clothes.

To save money on electricity, I like to pull my clothes out of the dryer when they are halfway dry. I give them a good shake, and hang everything I can on plastic hangers. I hang pants, skirts, shorts, even T-shirts. Most of them are dry by the next day. Be sure to use plastic hangers to avoid rust.

Then for the little things that are left over, like socks and underwear, I toss in a big dry towel for the last half of the drying time. The dry towel wicks out the moisture, and re-distributes it, so it actually takes less time to dry than it would without the dry towel. And since the dryer is now empty of most of the wet clothes, I am saving even more drying time, and saving more money!

There are some added advantages to hanging damp clothes. I like how some things like T-shirts come out as if they have been pressed. It's faster to hang T-Shirts than it is to fold them. And they stay nicer looking hanging in my kids' closets, instead of getting crushed in the drawers!

I remember when my oldest son first started dating, one girl's mother said, "He always looks so crisp and pressed!" I never pressed his T-shirts or jeans. But by hanging them halfway dry, they always have a crisp, pressed look.

"Oh yes, I've been slaving over a hot iron all day!"

Ha!

Keep Your Freezer Filled—And Not Just With Food!

When the weather gets warmer, a power outage can be devastating to the food in your freezer—and by extension your pocket book. So to get a jump start on those extra hot days, be sure to protect all that good food in your freezer now before it's too late. Here are two things that are simple to do, and can prevent a lot of damage in the event of a power outage:

1. Buy a freezer alarm. In the summer, and at all times of the year, you should have a freezer alarm in place. This should guard against accidental defrosting. A freezer alarm will usually have a temperature sensor inside the freezer, with a display outside of the freezer. If the temperature begins to climb, a loud alarm will go off.

Freezer alarms are easy to install, usually with no tools required. Some even include the batteries and sell for as low as $10.

2. Fill your freezer. A full freezer takes less energy to keep cold than a freezer with a lot of cold air. A full freezer will also stay cold longer if you have a power outage. If you have any empty space in your freezer, fill empty plastic milk cartons with water and freeze. It's easy to pull them out to make room for food if necessary.

Keep Ice Chests Cold

I like to wash, then fill empty plastic milk cartons with water to keep in our freezer. So we always have frozen milk cartons on hand for our ice chest when we go on a picnic or for camping in the summer.

Using frozen milk cartons is less messy and cheaper than buying ice for ice chests. Plus as it thaws, it's nice to have some ice water to drink.

We do the same with plastic soda bottles and water bottles. Even for day trips, it's convenient to be able to pull out some frozen water bottles to keep in a small ice chest for the car. Then we even throw in some string cheese that we bought with our coupons and other snacks for the road. Everything stays nice and cold, and there's no water damage from the ice, since the ice is all neatly packaged.

Frozen Casseroles For Camping

Sometimes it's nice to take one night off from cooking when we go camping. So in the weeks before the trip, I will make an extra casserole and freeze it. It's as easy to make two casseroles as it is to make one, so I'll make one casserole for my family at home one night, and a second for the freezer.

If I make lasagna, for example, I will make an extra batch in a disposable aluminum pan, and wrap it in several layers of aluminum foil. Then I freeze it. For the camping trip, this frozen lasagna goes in the ice chest. It helps to keep all the other food cold, and when it gets into about the second or third day, it begins to thaw. At that point, we'll put it on the barbecue on a low heat and covered. In about an hour, it's ready to eat.

Now that's one easy camping meal! It kind of gives me one night off from having to make dinner. Toss up a salad and you're done! Now that feels like a real vacation!

Turn Key Dinner

My son gets home from school at 3:00 o'clock. Since I work at home, my goal is to shut down my computer just before 3:00 p.m. Then I like to make an after school snack for him and sit and chat.

I like for him do his homework in the kitchen while I prepare our "Turn Key Dinner." Yes, that means I start dinner at about 3:15 p.m. Even though we like to eat dinner at 6:00 p.m., I get most of the preparation out of the way while he is in the kitchen with me. This way, I can be in the kitchen visiting with him, ready to answer homework questions, and all the while, I'm getting the bulk of the dinner preparations finished.

Here's a typical example of how a "Turn Key Dinner" would work by starting at 3:15 p.m.:

3:15 p.m. I wash and cut the fresh vegetables and place them in the pot with water, the steamer basket and the lid. I don't turn it on yet. (Takes about 10 minutes).

3:25 p.m. I wash the potatoes, wrap them in foil and put them on a baking sheet. I set that in front of the oven. But I don't cook them yet. (Takes about 5 minutes).

3:30 p.m. I cut a French bread loaf down the middle and place it on a baking sheet. I spread soft butter on it, sprinkle with garlic powder, and parmesan. I cover it with plastic wrap and set it aside. I don't cook that yet either. (Takes about 5 minutes).

3:35 p.m. I pull out my chicken that I had thawing in the sink. I wash it, trim it and rub it with seasonings. Then I wrap it back up and put it in the fridge. (Takes about 5 minutes).

Everything above takes me about 25-30 minutes. If I have finished all the preparation, and my son is still doing homework, I may do some deep cleaning on the microwave, fridge, or stove, while enjoying being with him.

Usually by 4:00 p.m., he is finished with his homework. Most often, he wants to play basketball with the neighbors, or ride his scooter or some other "boy thing". I give him a hug, and he is off to play. I head back to the office for about another hour.

4:50 p.m. I go back to my "Turn Key Dinner." Most all the preparation is done. I just need to start turning things on! I preheat the oven and then start setting the table.

5:00 p.m. I put the potatoes in the oven. And put the chicken on the rotisserie. (Takes about 10 minutes).

5:10 p.m. I'm back in the office. I work about another half hour.

5:45 p.m. I turn on the vegetables and preheat the broiler for the bread.

5:50 p.m. I put the bread in the broiler, and finish setting the table.

6:00 p.m. Dinner is served!

I love "Turn Key Dinners." At dinner, I always feel so relaxed. Because everything was done ahead of time, it almost feels like someone made dinner for me! And the best part is I get to spend time with my son. And I can also get more work done in the office while he is out playing.

OK, I'll admit—sometimes after 5:00 p.m., I just sit down and play the piano instead of going back to the office. After all, I should be off the clock after 5:00 p.m. anyway!

You can come up with lots of ideas on how to make your own "Turn Key Dinner."

In another amazing money saving book, "Shop Smart, Save More", I go deeper into how to save on groceries, from shopping smart to money saving cooking, culminating with good food on the table, and a happy cook.

I can save money, and I like to think I even do it gracefully. It's in my DNA, but more importantly, I have learned that I can live with grace and joy in both good times and bad. My Dad would often call out, in the midst of raucous family gatherings, paper airplanes littering the floors, and grandkids recovering from hours of merciless tickle fights, "Are we having fun yet?" Yes, we are!

About the Authors

TERI GAULT is founder and CEO of TheGroceryGame.com, a leading grocery savings website in the US. Teri's systematic savings approach kept her family afloat during times of financial hardship and ultimately led to their success. She has dedicated her life to helping other families thrive and prosper. Teri shares savings secrets in her first book, *Shop Smart, Save More*, written with Sheryl Berk and published by Harper Collins. She is currently working on a third book, *31 Days to Save*, coming soon!

PAUL JOSEPH GULINO is an award winning author, whose book, *Screenwriting: The Sequence Approach* has been adopted as a textbook at schools and universities around the globe. His credits include two produced screenplays in addition to numerous commissioned works and script consultations, and his plays have been produced in New York and Los Angeles. He taught screenwriting at the University of Southern California for five years, and since 1998 has taught at Chapman University in Orange, California.